Change and Effectiveness in Schools

SUNY Series

FRONTIERS IN EDUCATION

Philip G. Altbach, Editor

The Frontiers in Education Series features and draws upon a range of disciplines and approaches in the analysis of educational issues and concerns, helping to reinterpret established fields of scholarship in education by encouraging the latest synthesis and research.

Other books in this series include:

Class, Race, and Gender in American Education
—Lois Weis (ed.)

Excellence and Equality: A Qualitatively Different Perspective on Gifted and Talented Education
—David M. Fetterman

The Curriculum: Problems, Politics, and Possibilities
—Landon E. Beyer and Michael W. Apple (eds.)

Change and Effectiveness in Schools

A CULTURAL PERSPECTIVE

GRETCHEN B. ROSSMAN
H. DICKSON CORBETT
WILLIAM A. FIRESTONE

State University of New York Press

This publication is based upon work performed by Research for Better Schools, Inc. under a contract from the Office of Educational Research and Improvement, U.S. Department of Education. However, the opinions expressed herein do not necessarily reflect the position or policy of the Office of Educational Research and Improvement, and no official endorsement thereof shall be inferred.

Published by
State University of New York Press, Albany

For information, address State University of New York
Press, State University Plaza, Albany, N.Y., 12246

Library of Congress Cataloging in Publication Data

Rossman, Gretchen B.
    Change and effectiveness in schools: a cultural perspective /
Gretchen B. Rossman, H. Dickson Corbett, William A. Firestone.
        p. cm. —(SUNY series in frontiers in education)
    Includes index.
    ISBN 0-88706-725-5. ISBN 0-88706-726-3 (pbk).
    1. School improvement programs—United States—Case studies.
    2. High school teachers—United States—attitudes—Case studies.
    3. Social values—Case studies.
    4. Educational anthropology—United States—Case studies.
    I. Corbett, H. Dickson, 1950-
  II. Firestone, William A.
III. Title. IV. Series.
LB2822.82.R67 1988   87-33539
370.19—dc19   CIP

Contents

Foreword

A prime reason for understanding the connection between culture and the process of educational change is our interest in enhancing the effectiveness of schools. We should not forget this point. Rossman, Corbett, and Firestone certainly do not as they relate their "Stories of Three Schools," interesting in themselves, but told to provide concrete cases for illuminating the connection between culture, change, and effectiveness.

Though I am not persuaded that there is, or ever will be, a formula that can insure successful efforts to change schools, I do believe there is lore—"knowledge or wisdom gained through experience"—in abundance that can sensibly inform these efforts. Rossman, Corbett, and Firestone have written a book that abounds with such lore. Shunning the formulaic, the pat answer, the oversimplified list of guidelines, they offer us a richly rewarding discussion of culture and change that can help those who aspire to modify what goes on in schools.

It would be a considerable achievement if this book succeeded in conveying one fundamental notion that most often is honored in the breech: in every school a status quo prevails that can be designated a school's "culture," that is, its patterns of belief and practice that are "normal." Even granting some degree of discontent to a school's students, educators, or parents, they mostly accept those norms incorporated as the status quo. Thus, they seldom are eager candidates for reform. To ignore the implications of the fact that a school has a culture in place, and thereby overlooking how suggestions for change can be perceived as threatening, is to court failure, notwithstanding the wisdom of the proposed changes and the sincerity of their proposers. The authors do not shock us with their conception of culture and change. It has the ring of self-evident truth, which is to say that it squares with our sense of things. But how often do change agents heed it? Perhaps they will after reading the authors' fine explication and elaboration.

That we all esteem some beliefs, norms, and expectations more highly than others is also in the self-evident category. The authors draw our attention to this truism with their dichotomous labelling of norms as "sacred" and "profane." Sacred norms are "essentially immutable," while profane norms are "more susceptible to change." More than merely useful, it is critical for change agents to be aware of this distinction as they consider the substance and process of their change efforts.

Because conceptions of school effectiveness are embedded in those core values marked "sacred," and because core values vary from school to school, it is clear, as the authors tell us, that we should not be optimistic about "the success of current reform efforts to establish standardized measures of effective school performance." I thought about this observation as I read the three case studies, was forcibly reminded of how very different American high schools are, and considered this diversity in the context of today's numerous uniform state and national proposals for reform.

Following the three cases, the book closes with chapters on "Culture and Change" and "Culture and Effectiveness" that bring home, in insightful language, various attributes of change, for example, that it can be "a dollop of hand-slapping, and a heavy dose of symbolic activity"; that it proceeds with a "give and take among conscience, intention, and actions"; and that "the difference between behavior and cultural change becomes the difference between a momentary aberration and lasting reform." Clearly aware of the variable expressions of effectiveness extant in our schools, the authors conclude with an extensive discussion of effectiveness that centers on the concept of growth.

This, however, is not their last word, for the book actually ends with an appendix called "Research Methods" that must not be overlooked. This is a chapter-length statement that responds, in effect, to the reader's question about any book: "To what degree can we trust what we read in it?" "By and large, without reservation," is my emphatic reply. The nature and magnitude of the authors' time on the task of data collection is impressive; indeed, their procedure is a model worthy of emulation. I am persuaded that responsible qualitative researchers ought to provide comparable characterizations of their research procedure so that the readers of their outcomes can grasp how they came to know what they know.

We have in this book a valuable general organizing conception—culture, a set of case studies that take us graphically from the general to the particular, and a culminating discussion that returns us to the general. As a bonus, we get a first-rate discussion of the authors' research procedure. The result, in my view, merits congratulations.

Alan Peshkin
Champaign, IL

Preface

This is a book that probes deeply into schools' complex norms, beliefs, and values. The book metaphorically draws on a distinction borrowed from the sociology of religion to depict one of the variations in shared expectations for behavior that we found in three high schools. "Sacred" norms are those principles guiding professional behavior that establish meaning in teachers' work lives, that embody their purpose for teaching in their respective settings. As such, these norms are immutable; staff simply cannot imagine operating satisfactorily under alternatives to these principles. "Profane" norms, on the other hand, govern behavior less central to one's professional raison d'être. Usually supportive—and occasionally symbolic—of the sacred, these expectations are susceptible in varying degrees to improve knowledge and/or influence attempts. This is not to imply that altering profane norms is easy, only that it is ultimately possible. Indeed, resistance and anguish still accompany such changes. However, school improvement projects that impinge on the sacred reveal the point at which staff feel compelled to remove themselves from the setting, either actually, or psychically, or both.

The stories of these three high schools are integral to understanding school improvement, primarily because high quality ideas and sophisticated processes cannot succeed if divorced from knowledge of a school's culture and because success as defined from an outside agency's perspective may not correspond to the staff's definitions. Our purpose is to illustrate significant ways in which school culture can vary in schools, to detail its interaction with improvement efforts, and to depict competing definitions of the efforts' effectiveness—in essence, to discuss the relationships among culture, change, and effectiveness.

Acknowledgement must be given to the staffs of the three high schools. They opened their work places to us for a full year and suffered a multitude of requests for interviews, observations, and "chats". Intensive, qualitative studies are possible only through the gracious consent of the researched; and for granting their's, we are greatly indebted to the Monroe, Westtown, and Somerville (pseudonyms all) teachers, administrators, and students.

When we began this project, we all worked at Research for Better Schools (RBS), the mid-Atlantic Regional Laboratory funded by the U.S. Office of Educational Research and Improvement. Dick remains at RBS, Gretchen now teaches at the University of Massachusetts in Amherst while Bill is at Rutgers in New Brunswick, New Jersey. However, throughout this project, RBS proved to be a supportive and nurturant institution in which to work. Special thanks goes to our colleague in the Applied Research Group, Bruce Wilson, who paved our way into one of the sites and lent a ready ear to ideas about why what we were seeing there was happening. We also extend our appreciation to Elaine Krolikowski and Arlene Ziviello for professionally enduring repeated rounds of word-processing revisions.

Finally, we acknowledge Lois Patton, Editor-in-Chief at SUNY Press, for encouraging, supporting, and thoughtfully critiquing this project.

August 1987
GBR, Amherst, MA
HDC, Philadelphia, PA
WAF, New Brunswick, NJ

1

Introduction

This book describes the responses of three different schools to efforts toward change. In one high school, teachers embraced a new instructional model with graceful acceptance and occasional enthusiasm. In another, many teachers responded with frustrated anger to a program intended to improve students' basic skills. And in a third, the introduction of a districtwide emphasis on writing instruction was greeted with scorn by several influential teachers. What accounted for these differences? Why did teachers respond so variously to new programs or activities that promised to improve instruction? How did they interpret the intent of a program and decide on its appropriateness for their classroom, for the students they taught, and for the community the school served? What were the norms, beliefs, and values that were implicated when change confronted teachers? Which of these norms, beliefs, and values obtained for all teachers, and which were idiosyncratic to one high school or one group within a school?

Understanding how teachers respond to change is central to the problem of improving schools. As Fullan (1982:107) points out, "Educational change depends on what teachers do and think—it's as simple and complex as that." Three perspectives on planned change and teachers' contribution to it have evolved over the years: the technical, the political, and the cultural (House, 1981; Tichy, 1983). The technical perspective emphasizes a rational approach to improving professional practice and rests on the assumption that increased knowledge and technical assistance produce change; that is, teachers will accept a well-designed product that can be shown to improve instruction. The political perspective recognizes that this process is infrequently so straightforward and harmonious. It assumes that teachers, administrators, and others have interests that sometimes diverge and that all parties use the power and influence at their disposal to shape new programs. The cultural perspective stresses the importance of shared norms, beliefs, and values among practitioners and the symbolic meanings they attach to efforts toward change—a tacit, murky, and subjective side of social behavior. From this point of view, the frequent failure of educational innovations stems from the cultural conflicts between teachers and the technocrats who design and lead the implementation of those innovations (Wolcott, 1977). The shift in focus among the perspectives is "from the innovation, to the innovation in context, to the context itself" (House, 1981:28)

This book applies the cultural perspective to the study of planned educational change, for two reasons. First, although researchers have used all three perspectives to understand change over the last twenty years, the technical and political perspective predominate (Firestone and Corbett, 1987). This study is an attempt to increase knowledge about the more neglected, normative contexts of schools. Second, as Sarason (1971) forcefully argues, accustomed patterns of behaving and believing in large part determine teachers' responses to innovative ideas. Understanding these regularities in schools— their cultures—can help clarify the success, failure, or mutation of planned efforts toward change.

The thesis of this book is that the acceptance of improvement projects at the building level and the "effectiveness" of that school depend in profound ways on the existing school culture. The introduction of planned change challenges the status quo and instigates staff members to compare their current cultural content with that embedded in the new activity. Staff members respond to the innovation according to how well the proposed changes fit with the culture in terms of what is good and true. That being the case, it is critical to understand not only the dynamics by which school cultures shape initiatives toward change but also the normative content of those cultures, how malleable they are, and how cultural definitions of acceptable and valued behavior are distributed within a school. At the time they were studied, the three high schools whose stories are told in this book were in the midst of change (deliberately defined broadly; see the appendix for selection criteria); and in the minds of those who initiated the changes, the activities represented a quest for "improvement." The research tasks were to describe the cultures in the high schools and to document how those cultures accepted, deflected, modified, or rejected the initiatives.

THE CENTRAL ARGUMENT

The research examined patterns of similarities and differences among teachers' normative systems in each school. The purposes were to identify commonly held norms that were school-specific as well as cultural differences among salient intraschool teacher groups and to track the effects of culture on specific initiatives. As the reader becomes immersed in the stories of Monroe, Westtown, and Somerville, it is useful to keep in mind that the journey has a conclusion. This conclusion will be a series of statements that characterize the makeup of a school's culture and that depict the interaction between the culture and toward change. The statements are based on the cases but move the ideas to a more general level.

Each case uniquely contributes to the evidence supporting the central argument of this book. For example, two cases may illustrate opposite sets of conditions from which the reasonable inference could be made that other schools fall somewhere in between; one case may illustrate the consequence of the presence of a condition, another may reveal a different consequence flowing from the absence of that condition, and all three may point to the same result from the presence of a particular condition. Certainly such evidence does not constitute proof, but the data are strongly suggestive. As a result, the statements should be considered as the beginning of a theory that accounts for school-to-school differences in culture and faculty responses to planned changes.

The essence of the argument is as follows:

- A school's culture, the set of shared expectations about what is and what ought to be, derives from both the more distant external environment common to most schools and the local setting.
- Schools vary in the uniformity of their culture, that is, the extent to which norms are widely known and followed.
- Norms vary in the extent to which staff members perceive them as alterable.
- The aversion to change varies with the character of the norms challenged and the newness of the challenges.
- Behavioral change is possible through frequent communication of new definitions of what is and ought to be and close enforcement of those expectations.
- Behavioral change may be a preliminary to cultural change, but it does not insure acceptance of desired new norms.

Embedded in these statements are implications for school effectiveness. Essentially, definitions of effectiveness flow from a staff's core values. These values, of course, vary from site to site, and the variation bodes poorly for the ability of current reform efforts to establish standardized measures of effective school performance.

SCHOOL CULTURES

A cultural perspective on organizations, although not new, has currently taken on considerable popularity (see, for example, Deal and Kennedy, 1982; Tichy, 1983; and Schein, 1985). The resounding success of *In Search of Excellence* (Peters and Waterman, 1982) suggests that, apart from its faddishness, the concept of culture sensitizes and draws attention to certain aspects of the organizational process that have been neglected—notably the subjective, the symbolic, the tacit, and the normative.

What is the culture of an organization? The definition relied on in this study has two major facets. The first is that culture describes the way things are; it interprets events, behaviors, words, and acts—and gives them meaning. The second facet is that culture also prescribes the way people should act; it normatively regulates appropriate and acceptable behaviors in given situations. Thus culture defines what is true and good.

From a cultural perspective, organizational reality is viewed as pluralistic, subjective, and dynamic. Brown (1978:375) notes, "All of us to some degree design or tailor our worlds, but we never do this from raw cloth; indeed, for the most part we get our worlds ready-to-wear." The designing or tailoring of "our worlds" takes place within a context. People have personal histories and biographic idiosyncrasies; organizations also possess this baggage, which is carried in the memories of members and interpreted to newcomers as part of their socialization to the organization (Zucker, 1977). Culture becomes defined, then, as members react to, interpret, shape, and reinterpret the organization, its structure, processes, and events. This interplay of individual idiosyncrasy and collective meaning expresses itself in patterns of norms, beliefs, and values called "culture." In this study, Wilson's (1971:90) definition has been leaned on heavily: "Culture is socially shared and transmitted knowledge of what is, and what ought to be, symbolized in act and artifact."

This definition calls attention to an important aspect of the concept: culture is shared knowledge. It is carried in the minds of organizational members, learned by newcomers, and amenable to change, albeit with difficulty (Kottkamp, 1984; Schein, 1985). And this characteristic helps us determine the content of a culture—a particularly difficult problem to resolve. Both behavior (act) and its products (artifacts) carry cultural meaning—which is expressed, often unwittingly and implicitly, through language. The study of organizational cultures focuses on language; how people talk about their worlds, what they talk about and do not talk about, with whom, and where. Language is a crucial window for observing cultural beliefs and values at work. Thus the data in this research were obtained by capturing people's words about their work as they taught, met with others, talked with us, or wrote thoughts and directives on paper.

Influence of National and Local Setting

School cultures are not closed systems. In many ways they reflect the cultures of the larger societies of which they are a part. For instance, the emphasis in Japanese high schools on memorizing facts as preparation for the highly competitive national exams mirrors traditional societal values of diligence and conformity. The many electives and choices available in American high schools derive from the value placed on individual freedom and expression (Rohlen, 1983).

Societal influences are built into a school through both institutionalized expectations for behavior and socialization to educational occupations. Salient expectations are expressed through standardized rules or classification systems that obtain in the larger society (Meyer and Rowan, 1977). These rules are sometimes taken for granted, but they are often backed by public opinion or force of law. Schools incorporate these norms into their operation to demonstrate compliance with societal beliefs. The "comprehensive high school," with its mixture of programs for college-bound, vocationally oriented, and other students in the same building, is a form that highlights the values of choice and equality. The recent rise of requirements that high school students pass minimum competency tests to graduate represents the introduction of a new structure emphasizing rationality and accountability in American high schools.

Occupational socialization processes also give a certain similarity to patterns of school life. For example, Lortie (1975) depicts three teacher orientations to the occupation and ties their development to structural conditions faced by all practitioners. He argues that conservatism, individualism, and presentism have their roots in uncertainty about performance assessment, an incentive system emphasizing psychic rewards, and a "front-loaded" career pattern. Likewise, Sarason (1971) addresses nationwide practitioner responses to generic innovations such as the "new math." In this instance, regularities in the way teachers teach and view their professional purposes did not fit well with the methods implied by the innovation. The consequence was that the theory contained in the "new math" looked strangely like the "old math" in practice. From these angles, a school is a school is a school.

Whether one emphasizes the specific characteristics of a given school or generic characteristics it shares with other schools is a matter of figure and ground. On one hand, schools look, feel, and even smell alike. Instruction in one setting closely resembles instruction in other settings. Indeed, a major research thrust in education in this country over the years has been to capture the universal conditions of schooling, and several of the landmark works in education have emerged from this effort (such as Goodlad, 1984).

On the other hand, the effective schools movement—whatever else it may have done—has put the spotlight on school differences. In the special situations that run through this literature, local influences clearly have entered the mix of factors affecting a school's purposes and operation. Lightfoot's (1983) portraits of "good" high schools are particularly illustrative of the variety that ensues from a setting's input. Tradition, leadership, community expectations, and critical events all combine to infuse idiosyncratic elements into a school's culture. Similarly, Metz's (1978; 1986) studies of middle schools illustrate how these schools can differ in the value placed on order, in their emphasis on academic competition, in their views of students as active or passive learners, and in the implications of these differences for both program and everyday instruction. So by shifting the background and the foreground, the diversity of school cultures comes into focus.

Sharedness and Diversity

Rutter et al. (1979) argue that what sets a good school apart from mediocre schools is its ethos. A somewhat elusive term, *ethos* refers to the tone of the school, the "feel" one gets from being in it, or—using a more overworked word—its *climate*. What Rutter et al. (1979) mean is that there is a shared view of what the school is about and how people should behave to insure that this view materializes and is maintained. In other words, good schools have common ideas about what is and what ought to be, to recall Wilson's (1971) definition of culture. It matters, of course, what the content of these shared definitions is. A school is more likely to be a good one if staff members share a strong commitment to enabling all students to learn rather than an expectation that no one should stay in the building beyond student dismissal.

The degree of sharedness can vary in a school depending upon the particular expectation under consideration. Indeed, to understand the success of an effort toward change, it is as important to understand how widely norms are shared—the uniformity of the culture—as it is to understand the content of the norms. About norms, Wilson (1971:71) says the following: "In support of their values (conceptions of the good) men develop rules of conduct. Such rules, stipulating behavior commonly expected in a given role, are norms. Fixed in custom and convention, the norms of everyday life are less articulated in the mind than rooted in the heart." In developing a typology of cultural systems, Williams (1970) emphasizes their normative structure. Two key components of a culture's normative structure are the distribution of knowledge about norms and the extent of conformity to them. Thus, a more precise way to talk about a shared view is to say that most staff members know what the important expectations for behavior are, recognize to whom the expectations apply, and adhere faithfully to the expectations.

For these conditions to occur, there must be means for communicating the expectations, reinforcing them, enforcing them, and seeing them carried out. In Williams's (1970) analysis, the other two components of a culture's structure are the transmission and enforcement of behavioral expectations. To refer to a shared commitment then should conjure up an image of the considerable amount of discussion, observation, praise, and admonishment that lurks behind a school's ethos. In addition, and importantly, schools may have not only well-defined expectations for professionals and student behavior but also well-established patterns of rules, roles, and relationships for supporting them. In other words, the cultural fabric is a composite of loosely and tightly woven threads. At some points it is porous and easily loses shape; at others it is impenetrable and retains its integrity. Thus, a school's culture can be diverse and, consequently, selective. Important considerations concerning sharedness within an organization, then, include questions about what norms are shared, by whom they are held, and how effectively they guide behavior.

Schools with uniform cultural systems, that is, widely distributed and adhered-to expectations for what is and ought to be, face a serious problem with attempts toward change. Because well-established patterns of behavior are already in place, a proposed change *or* process of change that violates these patterns generates considerable resistance and turmoil. To an extent, this prediction of resistance to change belies the image of good schools being open to, and making use of, new knowledge of what constitutes good practice. But the two statements are not contradictory. The system's norms define where change is legitimate; and in these areas, such as the improvement of practice, change is welcomed and risk taking rewarded. Changes that challenge a shared foundation to the system—such as the commitment to all students' learning or the relationships felt necessary to pursuing that objective successfully—place it under attack. The moorings become dislodged, the anchors start to slip, and as a result uncertainty and anxiety emerge.

The three case studies upon which this book is based highlight the cultural diversity that can occur within a single setting. Teachers at Westtown, a medium-sized suburban high school, readily embraced proposed changes in instructional practice, more begrudgingly agreed to use new procedures to increase accountability, and dug their heels in as a response to adjustments in disciplinary practice. At a smallish urban high school, Monroe, several large pockets of teachers resentfully conformed to the letter of practices promoting basic skills instruction but adamantly resisted accepting the spirit of the changes. Somerville came the closest to exhibiting a uniform culture; nevertheless, the timbre of the acceptance given to norms concerning citizenship and order at this working-class urban high school dramatically thinned the farther teachers were from a central coterie of administrators and teachers. In each instance, the impetus to accept or resist change clearly had its origin in shared existing definitions of the true and good.

The Sacred and the Profane

Diversity obfuscates the relationship between culture and change and demands a closer examination of the conditions under which the interaction between the two takes on one quality or another. One particularly distinction concerning the normative makeup of a school's culture that will be discussed throughout the book is that between sacred and profane norms. This distinction denotes a qualitative difference among the set of norms that makes up a school's culture and is independent of how widely the norms are shared by staff members. Unlike the idea of sharedness, which can be discussed as a continuum, the sacred and profane constitute a dichotomy. The "sacred" is composed of essentially immutable norms; the "profane" is susceptible to change, with some norms more susceptible than others.

The two terms define completely different orders of reality, not just opposite poles of a continuum (Durkheim, 1965). The sacred is enduring, efficacious, and gives life its meaning (Eliade, 1959). For that reason, "as Durkheim points out, the ways in which we can approach the sacred are very limited. We must be diffident, careful, and respectful" (Gordon, 1984:96–97). On the other hand, the profane reflects the temporary adjustments to everyday life, the transitory side of existence. It is continually being redefined. As a result, the profane can be debated, altered, planned, and improved; the sacred simply is, and unquestionably adhered to. Members of the culture would be unable to consider the possibility of performing under alternative realities with any satisfaction.

But the distinction goes beyond one of inviolateness and

alterability. As Berger (1967:26) comments, "On one level, the antonym to the sacred is the profane, to be defined simply as the absence of sacred status . . . On a deeper level, however, the sacred has another opposed category, that of chaos." Thus, the inviolate nature of sacred definitions of what is and ought to be is the consequence of their being the normative anchors which keep the remainder of activity in the proper order. Their absence would create disorientation and a diminution of professional identity. Profane norms, although occupying strategic positions in the day-to-day world, do not have the broad meaning-establishing capability of the sacred. Together, both sacred and profane norms define the existing "regularities" in school life, that is, ingrained patterns of behaving and believing (Sarason, 1971).

These concepts derive from a long tradition of the use of social science in the study of religious phenomena (for example, Durkheim, 1965; Eliade, 1959). The sacred defines the realm of reality that gives life its meaning or purpose; it supplies stability. The profane, on the other hand, is worldly, mundane, and subject to redefinition (Gordon, 1984). Its transience is accepted; continual scrutiny of alternatives is legitimate, and even welcomed. It is not that the sacred's efficacy is supported by incontrovertible evidence, but that it simply has become defined as unquestionably true. Indeed, to justify the legitimacy of certain norms solely on the basis of some logic would be to suggest that change is possible if an improved logic can be offered. Apologetics and the sacred are incompatible. Profane norms may become acknowledged as "the way we do things around here," (Deal, 1982) but they are susceptible to improved knowledge.

The application of these terms to school culture is metaphorical. Certain norms in the universe of expectations for behavior within a school have qualities that resemble those of the sacred. For at least a subset of the staff members, the norms imbue organizational activity with meaning and are viewed as unalterable if staff members are to continue working in that setting. For example, most Westtown teachers believed that the classroom was the "capitol"—a term employed by a teacher to invoke the notion that the final arbiter of any decision, regardless of who made the decision, had to be what was instructionally good for students. The definition of what instructionally good practices were could change with available evidence but not the criterion that the decision should be in the best interest of instruction. This norm preserved the classroom from the intrusion of intramural and extramural political influences, despite occasionally intense pressure. The norm was also at the heart of the teachers' professional purpose and was the basis for dramatic reactions to challenges the teachers faced.

It is critical to note that resistance is not a sufficient indicator of the sacred. Certainly all challenges to sacred norms will be fought off resolutely; but resistance often greets adjustments in the profane as well. The difference is that attacks on the sacred represent attacks on professional raison d'être, on the cornerstones of teachers' constructions of reality. Shaking the foundation of these world views renders professional identities implausible and, in doing so, poses the possibility of a normless state of work where definitions of what is and ought to be are unclear. Tampering with the sacred is most likely to elicit responses such as "I will quit before I go along with that," or "they'll have to fire me first." Such anomic situations are debilitating. Teachers' behavior under these conditions may seem irrational and out of sync with what are viewed by others are relatively "harmless" changes. Regardless of whether the changes are benign or not, a carefully planned and rational process of change involving special technical assistance is not likely to be a very effective countermeasure. Indeed, attacks on the sacred will fail, either quickly in outright rejection or ultimately through the failure to gain a concomitant acceptance of the new norms. Without this corresponding internalization of norms, behavioral changes tend to disappear when special support systems are removed (Berman and McLaughlin, 1977; Corbett, Dawson, and Firestone, 1984; Huberman and Miles, 1984). It is unlikely that innovations that infringe on sacred norms will ever reach routinization, the final stage of the change cycle.

The sacred and profane distinction is not to be equated with that of the difference between important and unimportant norms. The profane can be an integral part of an organization's day-to-day operation. It is just that the profane is not inextricably embedded at the core of a staff's professional identity, and its alteration does not engender anomic reactions.

The distinction facilitates an understanding of the reaction of teachers to a variety of changes in the cases that follow. The terms provide an alternative perspective on behavior that from time to time resembled unreasonable stubbornness, an absence of vision, or commendable resoluteness. What appeared sometimes as resistance to an outside observer or administrator was often the preservation of a professional raison d'être for school staff members.

CHANGE: CULTURAL AND PLANNED

Cultural Change: Process and Influence

Culture tends to be a conservative, stabilizing force for any social system (Wilson, 1971; Hansen, 1979). Much cultural content has a deep sense of obligation attached to it. People act and think in certain ways because they feel strongly that it is right to do so. But culture also grows and changes as people come in contact with or create new ideas. Culture is, paradoxically, both static and dynamic. Conflict, dispute, disruption, or at least concern about the change ensues when culture becomes challenged. Organizational members' norms, beliefs, and values may be threatened because change requires modifying their behavior and their beliefs in some way. As Fullan (1982:26) comments, "real change, whether desired or not, whether imposed or voluntarily pursued, represents a serious personal and collective experience characterized by ambivalence and uncertainty." The status quo, or the established order of knowledge concerning what is and what ought to be, comes under dispute and the accepted meanings of everyday behavior are called into question. Three cultural change processes are relevant for a study of school culture and change: evolutionary processes, additive processes, and transformative processes (see Wallace, 1970:183–199, for a detailed discussion).

The first, evolution, is a steady state: new cultural norms, beliefs, and values are introduced at about the same rate that others fade away. Over time, the culture acquires new content, but the shift is not radical. As the new beliefs diffuse through the culture, some groups quickly accept them, and others are slower. The more complex the organization, the more likely there will be pockets of differential acceptance of the new cultural content (Wallace, 1970:184).

The second process, additive change, has the effect of modifying quite suddenly the norms, beliefs, or values in a particular domain of the culture. The new norm or belief then spreads to modify an entire set of beliefs. Historically, for example, new norms about who should be taught—for example, all children rather than just those of the wealthy—have lead to changed beliefs about the nature of education, teaching, and subject matter that now undergird the comprehensive ideal of American secondary education. Often, however, the champions of such changes do not intend to instigate cultural change and may not have thought through the cultural implications of their actions. Innovators who sought to introduce program planning and budgeting systems (PPBS) to schools, for instance, did not always recognize how their systems undermined teacher autonomy in the name of financial accountability (Wolcott, 1977).

The third process, transformation, occurs when one individual or a group deliberately sets out to change the culture. This process occurs when the culture is usually already under severe challenge and cultural expectations currently held have become discordant and dysfunctional, the organization has experienced a series of crises, or external agencies are demanding that the schools change. Some "trigger" (Tichy, 1983) touches off significant, often traumatic, change, which is achieved through the articulation of new cultural values by a leader or cadre of leaders.

Processes of cultural change may be evolutionary when new norms, beliefs, and values are introduced and discarded over time; they may be additive when new beliefs reverberate through and change a culture; and they may be transformative when cultural norms are challenged severely. These processes can be conceptualized along a continuum that reflects the degree of explicit, conscious focus on cultural change. Evolutionary processes are unplanned, initially diffuse, uncontrolled changes. That they are occurring is usually revealed through acute hindsight, although there is no shortage of futurists who project such trends. The length of time over which these changes come about, however, precludes a proactive involvement on the part of staff members working in a particular setting at a particular time. Additive and transformative processes, however, require some attention on the part of leaders or dominant coalitions to shape the new cultural content and to reinforce its expression. Additive processes typically do not focus explicitly on culture; instead, they involve the implementation of new programs, policies, procedures, or practices. Yet almost inevitably such planned changes implicate the existing culture, thereby posing the prospect of having to encourage acceptance of new definitions of what is and ought to be. Additive processes may not always lead to additive change. When there is too great a discontinuity between the proposed change and the existing culture—especially when the proposed change threatens sacred elements of the culture—the new practice or policy may have to be modified or ultimately rejected.

The problems and prospects of directing efforts of this sort have been the subject of the vast majority of educational studies of change over the last two decades; the next section of this chapter overlays a cultural perspective on this knowledge base in some detail. For the moment, it suffices to say that most of what has been learned about planning and directing change is contained in that body of information.

Transformation, by definition, is directed intentionally at achieving the acceptance of new cultural norms, for example, by defining and shaping a different school climate or tone. Although still sketchy, a growing literature has begun to address the topic of transforming organizational cultures. Three categories of influence strategies recur in the literature (see Schein, 1985; Tichy, 1983; Peters, 1978; and Pfeffer, 1981, for a complete discussion):

- attending to desired values and deliberate role modeling
- interpreting the symbolic elements of organizations, that is, stories, myths, mottos, and symbols
- shaping organizational systems to express cultural assumptions

The first two strategies stress specific cultural content through the repeated use of particular words, meanings, and phrases. Attending to desired values and interpreting the symbolic define and make manifest what matters. Through behaviors and language, preferred cultural content is expressed and conveyed to others. This "information context" (Pfeffer and Lawler, 1980; Manning, 1979) is an important source of knowledge for members because it provides cues about appropriate roles, acceptable behaviors, and acceptable reasons for those behaviors and makes certain information salient (Pfeffer and Salancik, 1978). In addition, rituals and ceremony (see Fine, 1984); organizational stories, sagas, myths, and legends (Ulrich, 1984); symbols (Deal, 1985); and language and ideologies (Clark, 1970; Peters, 1978, 1980) are all critical media for defining, shaping, maintaining, and breathing meaning into cultural acts and artifacts.

Much of the management literature examines how formal leaders use symbols and other media to support their goals and interpretations of what is important (Peters and Waterman, 1982; Schein, 1985). This interpretive activity can also become an arena through which conflicts between factions in an organization determine which definitions of what is true and good prevail. For example, the terms *curriculum alignment* and *teaching to the test* connote differently the legitimacy of altering curriculum content to better match the content contained in a particular test. Leaders can convey why an act or policy is important by what they call it, but staff members may redefine the same phenomena by employing different terminology.

The third strategy—altering systems—creates new interaction patterns in the organization, thereby breaking down traditional and habitual relationships. Accomplished by rearranging the composition of subunits or chains of command, redesigning committee membership or work teams, or flattening the organizational hierarchy, these dramatic changes help "unfreeze" the organization and create a climate of receptivity (Lewin, 1952; Schein, 1985). People come into contact in new ways; subcultural groups and the content of widely shared beliefs can now change.

School leaders have the authority to change some systems but not others. For example, large-city high school principals often have very little discretion in the faculty assigned to their schools. Although some maneuvering can be done, trying to alter the composition of the faculty and, through that mechanism, the extent to which certain norms are shared is not a particularly powerful avenue for change in those situations. Promotions, rewards, selection for compensated responsibilities, and membership in powerful cliques then become more potent mechanisms for signaling who and what matters. Curriculum content and testing procedures are other activities influenced more by officials higher than the principal. On the other hand, the principal has some leeway to establish procedures for staff decision making.

The changes examined in this study were mostly additive ones. The stories, therefore, revolve around the unanticipated cultural consequences of planned school improvement. School staff members tended to define the various alterations—both proposed and implemented—in technical terms. As a result, little deliberate attention to transformative strategies was in evidence, with the exception of the Somerville site. At the other two schools, the idea of transformation draws attention to the information context in which the improvement activities took place and serves as a lens through which to identify missed opportunities and misinterpreted intentions.

By introducing the sacred and profane into a discussion of additive change projects, this book poses the distinct probability that such processes, although typical of many change projects, will not lead to alterations in the sacred. Berger's (1967) analysis at the societal level would suggest that change in the sacred, if not a contradiction in terms, is a product of evolution through generations. Thus, group composition, and the concomitant balance between those holding a norm sacred and those that do not, may be the lever for change. Of course, the sacred may also serve as the building block upon which cultural changes are based. The evidence in the Somerville case will suggest this possibility.

Planned Change and School Improvement

Research studies on planned change and school improvement initiatives have documented score upon score of implementation failures. Despite a recent trend to report "good news" (for example, Crandall and Loucks, 1983), most researchers emphasize the difficulty of implementing innovations and keeping them in place after the initial attention and support declines (Berman and McLaughlin, 1977; Fullan, 1982). Despite the best intentions of university experts and the technical skills of instructional designers and material developers, many curriculum innovations simply have not found their way into the majority of classrooms (Welch, 1979).

Many reasons have been posited to account for this dismal portrayal of innovative efforts. Gross, Giaquinta, and Bernstein (1971) implicate poor administrative planning and the heavy logistical burden placed on teachers. Huberman and Miles (1984) point to the debilitating effects of giving insufficient time to teachers to learn new practices and of failing to plan for the later stages of the change cycle, particularly institutionalization. Other authors argue that teachers need to be given greater opportunities to participate in decision making related to the change (Berman and McLaughlin, 1977) or that principals need to be more dynamic leaders (Hall et al., 1984).

All of these are partial explanations rooted in technical or political perspectives on the process of change. They ignore the larger cultural dynamics at work. From a cultural perspective, the problem is that most efforts at change focus solely on *behavioral change*—alterations in discrete, observable, describable, and tangible actions—and the strategies that successfully promote them, and do not attend to the fit between those behaviors and the normative core of the school's culture. This core, including sacred elements not subject to modification, defines the existing "regularities" (Sarason, 1971) in school life, that is, the ingrained patterns of behaving and believing. Successful change must either accommodate that core or engage in the difficult enterprise of reinterpreting, redefining, and reshaping it. Doing so requires time, nurturance, and considerable application of power and creativity— qualities that are absent in many projects and policy initiatives described in the literature.

A cultural perspective on the process of change is informative particularly with respect to two issues the chapter will now address: the nature of teacher "resistance" and the relationship between planned change and effectiveness.

Teacher Resistance. When the study of planned change in education began, teacher resistance was seen as the major barrier to innovation (Giaquinta, 1973). The reasoning for this position was rooted in a social psychological tradition stemming back to the work of Lewin (for example, 1952), but it fit well with the then-current view of teachers as inherently conservative and unwilling to change without considerable prodding, coercion, or enticement (for example, Lortie, 1975). Resistance was viewed as irrational, and this irrational element was attributed to either a general personality trait or to a number of other traits, including intolerance for ambiguity, unwillingness to take risks, the strength of habit, personal insecurity, and the strength of the superego in the service of tradition (Watson, 1969; Zaltman and Duncan, 1977). The prescription for overcoming resistance to change was participation. Although studies claimed to have incontrovertible proof that participation routinely overcame resistance, the evidence on the point was at best mixed (Dunn and Swierczek, 1977; Giaquinta, 1973). How participation worked, however, was unclear. In spite of the democratic implications of the term, the emphasis tended to be more on management's use of group discussion formats to communicate effectively its vision of what the future should be than on shared influence (Coch and French, 1968).

Empirical studies of the implementation of innovations in education wrought havoc with this view of resistance as a pathology. In many cases, resistance was actually a rational defense against poorly planned and executed innovations. Administrators adopted innovations that did not clearly address a school's problems or help attain its goals; teachers did not receive adequate training in new and unfamiliar techniques, they faced standard operating procedures that were incompatible with those needed to support the changes, and they suffered from role overload and extra work (Gross, Giaquinta, and Bernstein, 1971). These circumstances prompted the suggestion that resistance could be overcome with better technical planning. Participation then took on a different purpose; it became a vehicle for upward communication from teachers to administrators to bring plans in line with reality. A great deal of recent research on planned change is intended to help administrators plan, implement, and routinize change more rationally and, in the process, remove the obstacles that add to teachers' work burden (see Crandall, Eiseman, and Louis, 1986). Currently, the term *resistance* has disappeared from the literature; the assumption seems to be that teachers are relatively neutral about the innovations they implement, that is, they are tolerant and willing to cooperate as long as the innovation in question does not make excessive demands on their time.

But are teachers that compliant and "reasonable" about administratively initiated innovations? The cultural perspective hints that they may not be. Instead, each school's culture specifies (1) ways that teachers should interact with each other, students, and administrators, (2) criteria of good and appropriate teaching, and (3) the ends to be accomplished through instruction. Teachers will evaluate an innovation according to how well it meshes with this existing culture. Innovations that further already established purposes will be welcomed, but others will be resisted. When any of the normative elements approach the realm of the sacred, they will be next to impossible to alter—especially within that cohort of staff members. And internalization of the changes by staff will be unlikely in the immediate future even if behavioral adjustments are in evidence. In sum, teachers' responses to an innovation may depend not only on the process by which it is planned and implemented—the concern of past research—but also on the congruence between its normative content and that of the school's culture.

Planned Change and School Effectiveness. The literature on planned change and on school effectiveness has become intimately intertwined in the last few years, and in many ways each reinforces the findings of the other (Clark and Astuto, 1984). Still, important differences in purpose remain. The research on school effectiveness is intended to help achieve specific ends related to educational equality, especially in urban schools seeking to improve their students' grasp of minimum literacy skills to the level of those attained in middle-class, suburban schools (Edmonds, 1979). Although contributors to this knowledge base do not object to having their work used to improve other schools, there is a clear focus on the poor and minorities.

The literature on planned change is somewhat more eclectic. At the service of policy makers, administrators, and school improvement specialists, this body of information is general enough to help incumbents of a variety of role groups solve a variety of problems. In some sense, it is content free. It attends to the process of change so that innovations intended to achieve a host of purposes can be implemented and institutionalized successfully.

But the process and content of change cannot be separated so radically. Are there general rules for implementing new programs that hold regardless of what the new program is intended to achieve, or does the purpose for which new policies and practices are designed affect what happens to them when they are put to use? It has already been suggested that the latter is the case. Both teachers and other members of the school community are likely to respond to a change in terms of its fit with the existing culture. Another way to approach the same phenomenon is to suggest that school cultures and innovations imply specific definitions of effectiveness. The success of an implementation effort will depend in part on the overlap of those definitions. To explore that possibility, it is useful to map effectiveness definitions in these schools. That is just one task to be addressed in the chapters that follow.

OVERVIEW

To insure that the schools selected for study were likely to be facing a reasonable amount of changes, site recruitment emphasized locating "improving" high schools. The assumption was that such sites would have considerable staff development, inservice, committee, and in-class implementation activities going on at any particular time. This activity would allow the observation of faculty responses to improvement "in process" rather than a less satisfactory reconstruction of a bygone era, especially one about which the myths have clouded the reality. In addition, research interests in the relationship between school culture and the currently-in-vogue school effectiveness movement reinforced the desire to examine schools that were in a position to focus realistically on a variety of effectiveness criteria. (The appendix details research design issues of site selection and study methods.)

The stories of the three high schools are contained in chapters 2, 3, and 4. Monroe High School was in a small city that had a declining industrial base. A trend of chronically low achievement test scores coincided with a shift in student population in the 1970s and became the target of a new superintendent who arrived in 1981. The cornerstone of the resulting "top-down" school improvement effort was an emphasis on basic skills instruction. The case echoes the importance of sacred norms in understanding teachers' reluctance to accept new practices. Monroe's focus on basic skills threatened teachers' commitment to their professional specialties; the more time spent on reading and writing, the less time there was to explore advanced levels of a particular content area. Teachers actively voiced their opposition while complying minimally with the letter of the mandates, thereby enabling themselves to remain true to their perspectives concerning the purposes of teaching. The Monroe story also underlines cultural diversity within a school in terms of which norms are shared by whom and provides a dramatic example of how behavioral, but not cultural, change is possible in spite of strong normative commitments to the contrary.

Westtown High School served a white-collar suburban community that was gradually shifting toward pale blue. The school had had a good reputation in the region, especially for its affective climate. However, declining SAT scores began to take the luster off this glow. A new principal was hired two years prior to the study to increase academic excellence, and did so through a broad assault on the curriculum, teaching practices, accountability, and discipline. The case introduces the sacred and profane in action. Initiative that threatened sacred norms in the school met with more than resistance; staff members experienced emotional, physical, and mental consequences as well. The case also illustrates that not all change challenges the existing culture, nor is culture inherently conservative. Instead, at Westtown, cultural norms concerning creativity and instructional soundness invited innovation in teaching practices.

Somerville High School was a community school situated in a close-knit, working-class neighborhood within a major urban metropolis. Not infrequently, two or more generations of the same family had matriculated there. Six years prior to the study, a new principal arrived and drew upon community norms of citizenship and order to build a school that meshed perfectly with local values. In spite of a certain amount of cultural baggage that is generic to all educators (Meyer and Rowan, 1977), the school became infused with a significant dose of local definitions of what was and ought to be. The culture in this school was the most uniform of the three studied. It was not surprising, then, to find a united response to recent school district efforts to standardize curricula and graduation requirements, initiatives that pushed this neighborhood school in directions contrary to its well-established purposes.

The three case study chapters do not adopt a common format. The uniqueness of each site's pursuit of its view of effectiveness demanded otherwise. One exception is that the cases all begin with a brief summary of the schools' contribution to the development of the six concluding statements listed above and explained more fully in chapter 5. This device is intended to orient the reader to the common themes underlying each of the rich, complex, and diverse stories.

Chapter 5 elaborates each of the propositions about culture and its relationship to change. In addition, it engages in some speculation about the conditions under which behavioral change leads to cultural change. Chapter 6 returns to the discussion of stipulative definitions of effectiveness and concludes with a challenge to policy makers, would-be agents of change, and those who are intimately involved in day-to-day school life. The challenge is to create, enact, and adopt changes that gently prod the organization toward some more desirable state while respecting the complexity, idiosyncrasy, and remarkable diversity of American high schools.

2

Monroe High School:
The Comprehensive Ideal
and Basic Skills Improvement

> Teaching used to be fun. In one classroom, you would have fifteen students, real A students, talking about ATP molecules and Kreb cycles. Now even the students who are supposed to be A students don't understand anything. [42]*

> I don't get all that many honor society kids . . . You can write your curriculum to kids with low reading levels. It doesn't bother me. I see more light bulbs going off that way. That's what I call teaching. [12]

A school's culture evolves as a composite of norms, beliefs, and values drawn from both the larger society and the local setting. The story of Monroe High School illustrates this mix of influences on school culture. The striking characteristic of teachers' beliefs in this site was the emergence of several perspectives on what should be taught and what should be expected of students. These perspectives reflected teachers' areas of specialization. They were local embodiments of the ideal of the comprehensive high school: the belief that the high school should serve the whole span of student abilities and prepare students for a wide range of future careers. This ideal

---

* Interview respondents in each site were numbered sequentially. The number in brackets refers to a specific person.

justified the departmental structure of the school, which in turn encouraged the several perspectives to develop.

Monroe teachers could not imagine deviating from these perspectives. When changes in the student body made acting on the perspectives difficult, teachers responded by rigidifying them, holding tightly to the views that provided their raison d'être. When administrators sought to redefine the school's mission to focus more on basic skills instruction, teachers actively voiced their opposition, complied minimally with the letter of the law, and essentially remained faithful to their initial perspectives. In sum, the idea of specializing and the accompanying perspectives had a sacred aspect: that is, the core of their educational purpose revealed an immutable quality. The sacred operated for these teachers not so much as a guide to making education more effective for the specific population of students in the school but as an anchor that defined one's place in the educational scheme. Challenges to teachers' views of the reality and rightness of their occupation took the form of an attack on what they held sacred; the inviolate was being treated as profane.

The Monroe story also illustrates that certain norms are not universally shared in a school. Four distinct perspectives were apparent among the Monroe teachers: academic, balanced, vocational, and psychological development. The beginning quotes in this chapter illustrate the differences between the first two of these perspectives. They tended to appear in specific departments. Except when there was competition for students, there was little conflict among teachers about these perspectives because teachers could act on their views within isolated classrooms. However, uniformly applied administrative mandates received different reactions among teachers depending on what each perspective defined as sacred.

Finally, the Monroe case suggests that behavioral change is possible in spite of strong cultural commitments to the contrary. In this school, the administration initiated a series of new procedures designed to help students pass state minimum competency testing requirements. These alterations were accomplished through frequent communication and monitoring. Teachers implemented these changes because they found ways to "render unto Caesar" that which was required, and test scores went up. However, as this chapter describes, they did so at a cost.

MONROE HIGH SCHOOL

From the outside, Monroe High at the time of this study looked like a typical suburban high school of the 1950s. The long, two-story brick building was fronted by an expansive, landscaped lawn. The front of the building was laced generously with glass and was very clean. The track, football field, and baseball fields were on a large lot across the street behind the building. Only in the back did one begin to see signs of an urban school—classroom trailers covered with graffiti and additional paint marks on the white cement foundations under the bricks. The building was constructed at the edge of Monroeville in 1957, when it served both the town of forty thousand and the surrounding suburbs. Subsequently the suburban districts withdrew from the agreement that sent their students to the high school, and the "best" black and white students in the city switched to private and parochial schools in the area. Enrollment dropped from a one-time high of over two thousand students to under eight hundred. Seventy percent of the current students were black, and 25 percent were Hispanic. About 70 percent of the students were poor enough to receive a free lunch.

Inside, the halls were clean and in good repair but never really empty. Crowded with students between periods, there were always a few when class was in session, moving slowly somewhere, chatting among themselves, teasing and being moved along by the security aides, who were mostly older women. One spotted a substantial number of pregnant girls and heard casual conversations about the health of students' babies. Classroom doors were locked, not, teachers said, because they were afraid of violence, as was the case in the early 1970s, but because they got annoyed when students who roamed the halls interrupted their classes.

The staff included just less than eighty teachers, five counselors, a librarian, one principal, two vice-principals, two disciplinarians, a general-purpose administrative assistant, and eight security aides. On the average, teachers had worked over ten years in the building, and only a third had worked in the building for five years or less.

Through the late 1960s and the 1970s, Monroe District experienced frequent turnover in administrators. Four teachers volunteered comments about changing superintendents. Eight specifically remembered four high school principals or more. This research began under one principal and was completed under a second. Many teachers expected administrators to come and go while they and their colleagues remained:

There have been so many changes in administrators in the last six or seven years. Each one comes in with a new thing that we've been forced to adapt to. You get the feeling that you'll last longer than the administrator. [13]

Since 1967 we've had eight different department heads and supervisors. Each has had different methods. The superintendents all want different curricula . . . We've had a variety of principals and a turbulent, chaotic atmosphere . . . The department staff stays. Everything else changes. That's why we stick together. We've weathered the storms. [05]

In 1980, Monroe District got a new superintendent who lasted longer than his predecessors and brought a level of stability to the district. This superintendent worked with the high school through a principal responsible for building operations and the associate superintendent for instruction, who, with a staff of subject area supervisors, was responsible for the quality of teaching in the district. The principal who was there for most of the research was promoted from within the district. This was her first principalship. The central office supervisors helped with staff supervision and evaluation. Seven supervisors worked part-time in the high school. They took on some tasks of department chairs and even vice-principals in other districts. Thus the central office had an unusually active presence in the school.

The superintendent faced two major issues related to the high school. The first was created by state policy. In the mid-1970s, the state legislature mandated a minimum competency test in reading and mathematics to be given to third, sixth, and ninth graders. Students had to pass the ninth-grade test to graduate from high school. When the test was first administered, scores from Monroeville schools were extremely low. The sixth-grade average was the lowest in the state. From the mid-1970s to the early 1980s, local newspapers periodically ran headlines like "City Students Falter at 6th Grade" and "Scores are Better But Still Too Low." In response to these low scores, the state department of education gave the district provisional rather than full certification and introduced an active program of monitoring which required state employees to visit the high school and check on its progress at least annually.

The Monroe District's plan for basic skills improvement began before the new superintendent's arrival, but he pursued it aggressively and expanded it to the high school. Moreover, even after the public attention concerning the first low scores had passed, he continued to push for improved basic skills instruction. As late as 1985, his annual mission statement had basic skills objectives that were publicized to district teachers. These objectives specified the number of students who would meet certain levels on the California Achievement Test and the state's competency test.

The second issue—low "morale"—was limited to the high school and received little publicity outside the district. The perception among teachers was that many of them were looking to leave the school:

I don't know what to do about the staff here. They're all waiting to retire. They don't give a damn. [31]

Good teachers are being put down a lot. They are not happy. Many of them are looking to move or retire. [48]

This perception was based on casual conversations among teachers, like the following taken from field notes: "One teacher said she would retire when she gets to twenty years because she will have a big enough pension. Another said she has twenty-five years now. She would quit but she needs to get to fifty-five years old to get the better benefits. She is forty-five." Eleven of the fifty-four teachers interviewed indicated that they would like to leave teaching. Only two wanted to move up to an administrative position. The rest wanted to get away from what they saw as a stressful or unrewarding job situation. Four of those said they were staying because changing jobs would mean a loss of salary.

Teachers' reasons for wanting to leave were summarized in the following observation:

Staying here will kill me eventually. There's so much paper work. It's always due yesterday. You're constantly being watched, observed, and scanned. There's too much pressure . . . The kids are part of it too. Meeting their demands. You have to watch for cuts and behavior problems. Writing up cuts takes time. [56]

This comment pointed to two problems. One had to do with teachers' relations with students:

I see rudeness and defiance rather than "I'm a sick kid. Help me." . . Anymore I can't come up and put my arms around a kid and say, "What's wrong?" [50]

Kids get on your nerves. Their language. Their arguments. [07]

Information sails over their heads . . . I got the answer that Hitler led the Jews out of the promised land. Hitler wrote the Declaration of Independence. [46]

A third of the teachers (eighteen out of fifty-four) made some complaint about the students they taught.

Even more teachers complained about how they were treated by the administration. Over half the teachers (thirty out of fifty-four) volunteered some complaint about the building or district administration. They complained about special tasks that they disliked and lack of administrative support. They inferred negative administrative attitudes towards themselves to which they reacted very strongly:

Downtown treats us like garbage! [35]

Teachers are willing to do more than we're told to do. We're not given enough initiative. We're supervised to death. There's a one-way pipeline from downtown and the building administration to us. [06]

We are undermined on discipline. Take the no-hat policy. The administration makes a big deal about it. I wouldn't let a student in class with a hat on. He went to the office. The principal said, "Oh let him in as long as he doesn't wear it." I'm trying to follow their rule. [51]

Tensions had risen to the point that the central office administration was as angry with the teachers as the teachers were with them. One important central office administrator made the following observation:

This faculty had defeated a lot of people . . . Basically, they want to be left alone. They don't realize that [the state competency tests] are facts of life. They want to be left alone . . . It's like if you get on a plane to California and the pilot says we aren't going to California. We'll go to Florida. That's what they want. [22]

This last comment suggests that the efforts to increase students' basic literacy had increased the strain between teachers and the district office. That was in fact the case. To understand why it was so, it is useful to first explore the teachers' sense of purpose and then the district's program.

PERSPECTIVES ON PURPOSE

The tensions between teachers and administrators stemmed in large measure from fundamental disagreements about the high school's priorities. Responding to state and community pressures to increase test scores, the superintendent stressed the importance of increasing basic skills achievement. Few teachers shared this priority. Instead, they felt that they should teach their specialty. If that specialty did not bear directly on improving basic literacy skills, then the teacher should not be responsible for helping students learn them. One typing teacher expressed this view as follows:

> Our job is to prepare students for the business world. English should work on the students' reading ability, and the math department should work on math. Indirectly, I can help; but directly, no . . . I shouldn't have to teach basic skills . . . But I can tell who has low basic skills by how they proof. They're here to learn how to type. That's what I should teach. [03]

This comment also illustrated a problem with this division of labor. Although most teachers were not responsible for basic literacy instruction, the lack of basic skills impeded their efforts to teach their fields.

Rather than focusing on basic skills instruction, teachers held four different perspectives about what their educational purposes should be. These perspectives were academic, balanced, vocational, and psychological development. These perspectives defined sacred aspects of teaching—primarily the idea of specialization—and teachers went to great lengths to act in accordance with them, as the bulk of this chapter will show. Before doing so, it is necessary to describe these perspectives and trace their roots.

Perspectives on Teaching

Teachers holding the *academic perspective* were committed particularly to their subject matter, specifically in introducing students to the more advanced aspects of their respective fields. For many teachers who articulated this perspective, their field had an intrinsic compelling appeal. They found the subjects inherently interesting and enjoyed working on the more challenging issues that were incorporated into the secondary curriculum. Thus, teachers reported the following:

> I enjoy calculus. I can work out Algebra II problems without doing the homework. I *have* to do the problems in calculus. I enjoy the refresher . . . When I get the answer right, I feel like the kids do. [27]
>
> I enjoy teaching classical literature because I enjoy it, and I think educated kids need it. [07]
>
> I like teaching the subject I love. I would prefer teaching at a higher level than I am now. I'd like to get into literature and character study." [16]

Teachers did not just enjoy their fields. They also believed that their special competence came from their knowledge of the subject matter and how to present it. They were wary of any definition of their task that required other kinds of expertise: "I am not a social worker or a psychiatrist. I'm not trained to work with traumas. I'm interested in academic development. That's why I'm in teaching" [09].

The academic perspective was found primarily among the teachers of the traditional college preparation subjects— English, mathematics, foreign languages, and science—although it was held by a few people in other fields. Generally, it was associated with an interest in preparing students for college. Since college preparation is an important and prestigious function for high schools, this perspective also had a certain appeal to administrators, as will be seen.

Teachers holding the *balanced perspective* were also interested in their subject matter, but not necessarily in teaching the advanced courses. The balance was between the interest in the subject matter and in the student, as the following comment indicates: "Geometry is my favorite . . .

[Another teacher] doesn't like geometry 'cause teaching proofs is tough to these kids. I don't get frustrated. I have tremendous patience . . . I like geometry and I like teaching geometry" [25]. Many of these teachers tried to make a reasonable accommodation to students who would not benefit from a heavily academic curriculum by finding what they could be taught: "I taught English . . . If students are prepared, English is more interesting, but students can't read so you have to work at an elementary level . . . It made better sense to work where they were" [37]. Not only were these teachers willing to teach a different intellectual content, but they were more patient when working with students on the behavioral prerequisites for instruction. According to one teacher, they were "elementary based. They were more willing to hound students to bring pencils and notebooks to class" [35]. Most teachers in the reading department (who referred to themselves as "elementary oriented") adhered to the balanced perspective, as did some teachers in the English and mathematics departments.

The *vocational perspective* was found among the teachers in the industrial arts, business, home economics, and even health and physical education departments. Teachers holding this perspective were less concerned with teaching advanced courses and saw those courses somewhat differently than did the academic teachers. Advanced vocational courses did not necessarily require higher intellectual skills or provide greater challenges to teachers. Instead, they were more practical and directly related to jobs. Thus, teachers in both health and home economics wanted to develop programs to prepare students more directly for work in fields related to their specialties: "I expect that Middle States will say that if [this field] continues, we will need a coop program. I'm ready. I hope they will let me run it" [12].

The *psychological development perspective* was very broad. It included an emphasis on developing self-esteem. "I work with their self-feelings. I want to drop History II and do more to prepare them for jobs. A lot of these kids don't think they're important. That's bad. I build up their respect" [48]. Another element was a concern with teaching students appropriate behavior. " I think social studies should be about behavior. If I saw my students hassling another teacher, I'd talk to them about their behavior. We talk about behavior a lot" [45]. These teachers were more likely to refer to a knowledge base that comes from understanding students than subject matter expertise. "Yes, we have knowledge. I bring in expectations for individualizing. For instance, I didn't push [a girl who thinks she is pregnant] because I knew about her problem" [54]. This more diffuse sense of caring for children's self-esteem and behavioral development was found primarily among the special education teachers and to some extent as a secondary theme among a few English and social studies teachers.

For the most part, teachers holding different perspectives were able to coexist peacefully because they had relatively little contact about instructional matters. There was a distinct element of tension and competition, however, between those holding the academic and the vocational perspectives, particularly between vocational teachers and the administrators and counselors. It inhibited efforts to broaden curricular offerings:

> [The districts' administrators] want to see themselves as running an academic school with a clientele that's not prepared for academic life. Any curricular movement towards anything else is defeated. We had a [content area] careers orientation program that didn't work . . . We wrote a proposal and got [equipment] but we never got a curriculum . . . There never was a commitment from the district. [31]

This tension also appeared in competition for students where teachers of the vocational and practical subjects felt overmatched by administrators and counselors. Four teachers explicitly described a double bind. They had to maintain adequate enrollments for their programs to continue. Yet, the brightest students were counseled away from their fields into college preparatory courses, and the students with academic deficiencies were unavailable because they were required to take remedial courses. During the research, specialized agricultural and graphic arts programs were eliminated for lack of enrollments. Shortly afterwards, in another context, the superintendent made a public commitment to keep more academic courses like calculus and advanced science courses in the curriculum even with very low enrollments.

Sources of the Perspectives

As suggested in the introductory chapter, teachers' perspectives on what they should teach did not develop out of "raw cloth." They were manifestations of larger currents in American society and were stimulated by the school's departmental structure, which was a reflection of institutionalized views about what high schools should accomplish. In spite of some dissent (Sizer, 1984; Boyer, 1983), the prevailing thinking in American high schools is still shaped by the ideal of the comprehensive high school. This ideal claims that the purposes of the high school should be broad enough to include students from the full range of races, economic backgrounds, and achievement levels in American society as long as they are between the ages of fourteen and seventeen. As a result, instructional goals are quite diverse.

Conant's (1959) popularization of this ideal specified three objectives for secondary education: education for citizenship, education for a job, and college preparation. These themes remain enduring threads in discussions of what high schools should accomplish. Since Conant's formulation there has been some shift in the purposes of high school with a tendency to give greatest attention to the students at the two ends of the ability continuum, the precollegiate and the special education students (Powell, Farrar, and Cohen, 1985). These developments provided the basis for three of the four perspectives identified in Monroe High:

The academic perspective, which reflected the college preparation objective

The vocational perspective, which reflected the vocational preparation objective

The psychological development perspective, which reflected the growing concern with students at the bottom of
the achievement distribution, especially those in special
education

The balanced perspective is perhaps appropriate for the vast
middle range of the ability distribution that Powell, Farrar, and
Cohen (1985) argue are poorly served by the modern high
school.

Although Conant's formulation makes college preparation
one objective among three, that theme has a special place in
thinking about high schools. Its history precedes that of the
comprehensive ideal. The earliest American high schools were
institutions to prepare elites for college (James and Tyack,
1983). The college preparation function expanded in the
postwar period as the proportion of teenagers going on to
college grew. This expansion was driven by the belief that
higher education would enhance opportunities for upward
mobility (Cohen and Neufeld, 1981). More recently, interest in
the most rigorous portions of the high school curriculum has
been enhanced by reports of a variety of commissions making
recommendations for the improvement of secondary education (for example, the National Commission Excellence in
Education, 1983). It is this pervasive interest in college
preparation and academic rigor that gives the academic
perspective such power among both teachers and administrators.

The comprehensive ideal is implicitly intended for a
student body with a wide range of abilities and future careers.
If anything, it underestimates the problems of the children of
the poor, who frequently lack the prerequisite skills to address
the curriculum objective inherent in this idea. Yet American
schools are becoming more segregated in terms of wealth, race,
and ethnicity (Abramowitz and Rosenfeld, 1978). Public
schools in major cities are increasingly filled with students
whose problems, aspirations, and out-of-school resources do
not fit the assumptions of the comprehensive ideal. The
comprehensive ideal offers no prescription for serving these
students.

Monroe High School became associated with the issues confronting a poor, minority student population in a dramatic manner. In the early 1960s, it had an integrated student body and drew a substantial number of academically able students from two suburban districts that did not have high schools. The transition from that period was a frequently retold story. The earlier period now seemed like a golden age to older Monroe teachers. Old-timers in the school reported that they could teach more advanced academic classes and had the reward of seeing a substantial number of their students go to better colleges and universities. This period was followed by "the riot years" from about 1969 to 1972 caused by racial strife between students. The schools were closed, frequently because of fights between black and white students. In 1985, teachers still talked about "the riot squads on the lawn" and the policemen who were unwilling to come into the school alone. They remembered the serious problems they had controlling their classes and achieving any instructional ends. This period ended when the two suburban schools stopped sending students to Monroe High and most of the white and more academically mobile black families in Monroe City began sending their children to private schools. Teachers believed that this change reduced the achievement level of the student body. One ending of this story was that "everything changed, and they left us with the dregs" [11].

The "Right" Kind of Students

Not all teachers viewed low-achieving students as the dregs. In fact, they varied substantially in their outlook, with some shunning low-achieving students and others welcoming them. These differences were related to their perspectives on teaching.

At the most exclusive extreme, some teachers only wanted the top track students, whom they viewed as sharing their interests. When teachers worked with these students, they looked for opportunities to enrich their curriculum in ways that allowed them to explore more advanced or esoteric subject matter. Thus, one senior English teacher researched little-known black writers of the 1930s in order to bring something different and more intriguing to his class.

These same teachers found the basic literacy classes repetitive and draining, lacking the stimulation of the more advanced classes:

> We don't teach the term paper to all students. We teach a term report to some 'cause they can't do a paper. A term report doesn't deal with a thesis. It's not much more than get a topic, gather information, and arrange it. Last year, I had two low eleventh grade classes. Out of fifty students, I was so angry, all but two turned in papers . . . When we did the outline I worked with each student individually to help write it. I write it with them. Sometimes, I'll actually write it. It's the worst kind of labor to go through that with forty-five or fifty kids. [11]

A few teachers were so angry that the "right" students were not available that they refused to recognize real signs of interest when they occurred. Even with a class that responded to a lecture and demonstration with curiosity, one teacher commented, "You have to keep your spirits up" [42].

Teachers evaluated students on two dimensions. The first was intellectual or academic performance. Here they usually identified the problems:

> Why should we remediate what should have been taken care of in elementary school? They shouldn't be here if they can't read and write. [56]

> You should be able to take things for granted that you can't. When I put the formula, area equals length times width, on the board and assume that students know what I mean when I substitute in numbers, I can run into problems. [06]

> In a college prep class, I have to show students how to do long division. I shouldn't have to. It slows down the good kids, and it slows down the work. [41]

The comment that a teacher was willing to teach "low-ability" students because he or she saw "light bulbs going off that way" was the exception to the rule among Monroe teachers. Fourteen teachers indicated that students generally lacked some academic prerequisites for what they taught.

The second dimension was student attitudes towards school and self-control. The issues could range from forgetting to bring pencils and books to class, through not doing homework, to disrupting the class. One teacher tried to understand behavior that was found to be disruptive:

> Their environments are mind boggling. [A girl] lives with her mother. There is another man in the house, but the mother is not married to him because she may get married to someone else. Yet there are step children. There are social complexities beyond my comprehension. In one class I had five pregnant girls. And you talk about intellectual development. It's absurd. The girls always had to go to the bathroom, and one had morning sickness. [09]

Others simply described how students' behavior made it difficult to conduct class:

> Most of them can do the work. They're immature . . . There are certain stories that some of them like, but their habits are chronic . . . Chronic laziness . . . They pick and choose a lot what they like. Vocabulary they don't mind, but very few will do the reading. [05]

> Attendance is another problem. A lot of kids don't come to school. School is not a priority. [36]

> Most kids don't want to work. They won't do homework. Even in the good classes. [28]

Twenty-two teachers saw these attitudes as a barrier to what they defined as appropriate teaching. Only a handful defined them as a problem to work on. "It's not what I teach them academically. It's what I teach them behaviorally. These kids are gonna get jobs. If they can learn responsibility and to control their emotions, that's the biggest thrust of special education. Life skills" [54].

These beliefs about students were examples of profane elements of the school's culture. The beliefs did not establish meaning for teachers' professional lives; rather, they flowed from the sacred, from teachers' views of their specialities. Indeed, there was a definite association between teachers' perspectives and their inclusiveness. Those who held the academic perspective were the most likely to be exclusive, to be impatient about students' intellectual skills and self-control. These characteristics were, after all, prerequisites for the kind of teaching they wanted to do. Those who held the psychological development perspective were generally the most patient, since part of their job, as they defined it, was to work with students on their behavior and to find intellectual content that was appropriate for them. The teachers with the balanced and vocational perspective typically fell somewhere in between. Some were willing to teach and reteach patiently, to teach to lower-ability students to see "the light bulbs going off," and to "hound" students about books and pencils. Others were nearly as impatient and frustrated as the academic teachers.

Beliefs and Instruction

The beliefs associated with the academic perspective—strong interest in one's subject matter and impatience with students' skill levels and behavior—were enacted in a number of ways. Some included adjustments of formal curricular and evaluation arrangements. The question these arrangements raised was how to respond to commonly held standards for high school performance. Curricular standards were reduced: "Once the school became predominantly black, the curriculum changed. I went to an all-black school, and they had high expectations for me there. I don't see how come a person doesn't expect the same thing from anyone as a black" [18]. The curriculum was usually adjusted through the selection of texts that were easier to read or the switch from term papers to "term reports" discussed above. The effect was often to ask less of the same content from students rather than to ask for something more instructionally appropriate.

Other teachers decided to maintain the grading standards they had used when Monroe High had a more diverse student clientele:

> We fail a lot of students. A couple of people have failed most students in their classes. The administration wants us to give them higher grades. The old-timers feel that if students get an A in a college prep class, they should do what the students did ten years ago, but the students are not as good and not as prepared. [41]

This response was limited to one department. Other teachers were more likely to pass students. Some, however, would speak of situations in which "if he receives a C, it's a gift" [05]. These teachers referred to the same standards as those used by the departments that failed most students, but they accommodated by scaling down. If the student did not misbehave in class, she or he was allowed to pass.

Within the classroom, teachers' frustrations came out in a number of ways. Some teachers made insulting comments to students:

> I hope that if I put the date for the War of 1812 on the test you'll all get it, but knowing some of you . . . [47]

> Some of you in here still can't plot a graph after we've been doing it for so many days. Some people can't even draw a straight line with a ruler. Would you believe it? Would you believe it!? [30]

Teachers who made these comments were likely to make a negative interpretation of student behavior even if positive ones were equally possible. When one student asked how one animal family inherited a characteristic from another family, the teacher said that the student took the idea of cross-species inheritance "literally"—prompting a spirited defense by the student—rather than noting the effort to draw connections between the current lesson and what had been taught earlier [42].

According to students, a second response was cryptic teaching, the failure to explain concepts fully and make sure that students understand:

> Some teachers give homework and don't ask for it or check it. They just go on to other work. Teachers who care check to see if you understand. They ask if you understand. [58]

> [A good teacher] is a person who gives you a picture of what she is saying. Some just take twenty minutes and say do your work. Then they get upset when you get a low grade. The better ones take the time to ask if you have questions. [59]

A third response was to get rid of unwanted students. One teacher reported the following:

> Some teachers send students down [to the office] for frivolities, things that should be handled in the classroom. You'd be amazed at the things kids get sent down for . . . a lot of trivial referrals and abdications. Some teachers are proud of it. They say, "I got rid of him fast." [35]

The disciplinarians in the school were overwhelmed with the number of referrals from teachers and ran a backlog of as much as two weeks, leading to complaints from teachers about lack of administrative support. Part of the backlog stemmed from some teachers' unwillingness to handle certain problems themselves. The principal devoted two staff meetings to workshops on how teachers could better handle disciplinary problems without referrals. Students were not just sent to the disciplinarians, however. The librarian complained that many were sent to the library; others went to the cafeteria; still others were simply allowed to roam the halls; and some left the building.

Harsh grading, insults, cryptic teaching, and sending difficult students out of class were not engaged in by all teachers. Some went to great lengths to avoid these activities. "I put paper down in front of students carefully. Otherwise, they will be insulted. I expect students to do the same with me. If a student pushes a paper at me and doesn't apologize, I won't pick it up until we clear it up" [35]. Where those activities did occur, they were enactments of teachers' frustrations, but they also added to frustrations by increasing the likelihood of teacher-student conflict, thus creating a vicious cycle.

THE BASIC LITERACY PROGRAM AND TEACHER RESPONSES

For most teachers, their perspectives provided an explanation for why they should *not* help students attain basic skills literacy; indeed, they were unwilling to adjust as the number of students who exhibited basic literacy problems increased dramatically. Eventually poor basic achievement became a publicly recognized problem. State competency tests publicized it, and state monitoring and public outcries created pressures to adopt a solution. The district did develop a program to address the problem. Teachers responded to that program in terms of their perspectives on teaching and their understandings of appropriate teacher-administrator relations. Many teachers objected on principle to the program, which violated their fundamental conceptions of what constituted good teaching. All teachers objected to the tactics used to enforce compliance. Yet limited compliance to the most visible, enforceable activities of the program was achieved. Moreover, test scores increased. To that extent the program was a success. This section describes the program and teachers' responses to it. It then explores why the levels of compliance observed were achieved and the relationship between the program and student achievement.

Elements of the Program

When the new superintendent began work in 1980, he found an outside consulting organization already working with the district on basic skills instruction. After examining that organization's approach, he made it the centerpiece of the district's program. It was introduced to Monroe High in 1982.

The consultants' approach stressed the strengthening of administrative monitoring and supervision to maximize teachers' effectiveness. It identified a number of key variables that could be manipulated to increase the quality of instruction and worked with the district to develop effective monitoring devices. The two variables that received the greatest attention in Monroe District were "time on task"—that is, the amount of time available for instruction—and "curriculum articulation," or the fit between what was taught and what was tested. The district introduced activities in both areas.

The time-on-task activity focused on classroom management. Initially, teachers received instruction on how to increase instructional time in their classrooms. The consultants gave a great deal of attention to measuring instructional time. The mechanism they developed was called the "scan." An administrator would come into a classroom for fifteen minutes. At regular intervals, she or he would note the number of students engaged in such on-task behaviors as listening to the teacher or working on exercises and such off-task behavior as getting out books, talking to other students, or looking out the window. A few simple calculations after the observation period gave the administrator the class engagement rate, which was shared with the teacher.

The consultants' theory also noted how instructional time could be increased by focusing on a number of schoolwide considerations. One could cut time spent passing in the halls by reducing the number of periods in the classroom day and by minimizing such classroom interruptions as PA announcements. However, during this study, no effort was made to change Monroe High's eight-period schedule with its frequent class changes. The number of PA announcements during class time varied during the observation period, but at the extreme there were as many as six a day.

The curriculum alignment activity began with a careful analysis of the school's curriculum. Departments were asked to compare what was taught with the content of the achievement tests used by the district and the state's minimum competency test. Teachers then rewrote the curriculum as a series of objectives to be met each quarter. These objectives were to be coordinated with the achievement and minimum competency tests. Departments that did not normally teach the minimum competencies were to incorporate activities related to them in their curriculum.

The district's curriculum alignment monitoring involved two separate documents to be completed by teachers. Before each quarter began, teachers were to complete a quarterly topic plan (QTP) indicating which objectives would be addressed, the amount of time to be spent on each, the materials used to work on the objective, and the dates by which work on each objective would be complete. These plans were reviewed by supervisors and returned to teachers. As each objective was completed, the teachers were expected to record on the QTP the "success rate"—that is, the number of students who got a C or better on a test related to the objective. The second document was the weekly lesson plan, which elaborated the QTP and indicated what the teacher would do each day. During classroom observations, administrators and supervisors would ask to see QTPs and lesson plans and would determine if in fact teachers were on the schedule they specified in the QTP. The administrators' rationale for emphasizing adherence to the schedule was that it insured that students were introduced to all the content on which they would be tested at the end of the year.

Although teachers came to see the scans and the QTPs as the core of the formal program, there were several other elements involved. First, there was a series of remedial reading and mathematics courses for students who did not pass the minimum competency test at the end of the ninth grade.

Students who continued to fail the test remained in these courses until the end of their senior year, and all ninth graders were required to take reading as well as English. Second, administrators and teachers worked to impress on students the importance of doing well on the minimum competency and achievement tests. School staff members reasoned that students did poorly on the tests partly because they did not think their scores mattered. As a result, administrators bombarded students at assemblies and through PA announcements with reminders of how important the tests were and that they could not graduate unless they passed the minimum competency test. These announcements reached their peak in the weeks before a test.

Finally, students were drilled specifically for the test. The district had access to old versions of the minimum competency instrument. In the weeks before the tests were given, English, reading, and mathematics teachers had students practice with old items. In 1985, when the state switched to a harder assessment instrument, a university professor developed a practice book for it. The district bought copies of it and had teachers in relevant subjects use them as the major portion of the curriculum in the weeks before the new administration date, even indicating that work in the book should supersede activities described in the QTPs.

This overview of the program highlights two important characteristics. First, the program was an effort to modify and monitor certain teacher activities, like their use of classroom time and the speed at which they covered a certain curriculum. Teachers were given considerable leeway in their initial planning, although drilling on the tests was mandatory. However, the administration monitored carefully to insure that plans were followed, and deviations from schedules had to be explained. From the administrative perspective, the program was an accountability mechanism to insure that teachers engaged in what were viewed as correct or appropriate behaviors. One key district administrator asked the following:

> When we do observations, how tough are we in holding teachers accountable for goals? When students don't do

well, they don't pass. When teachers don't do well, they
should get a poor evaluation and no salary increment . . .
If we as supervisors and principals don't hold the line,
we're in collusion with teachers for poor success rates for
students. [23]

Although this same administrator would have liked to have
teachers more accepting and enthusiastic about the program,
the bottom line was not intended to be attitudinal or cultural
change. The main concern was additive changes to insure that
teachers engaged in expected behaviors.

Second, the various parts of the program affected teachers
in different ways. All teachers were monitored through the use
of scans and QTPs, and most were asked to incorporate
activities to improve students' basic skills in their classroom
activities. Still, the burden of preparing students directly for
the achievement and minimum competency tests—whether
through the drill activities or through the regular curriculum—fell primarily on the twenty-two teachers in the English,
reading, and mathematics departments, about one-quarter of
the faculty. This time available for working on basic literacy
skills was limited because some of those teachers had courses
like calculus or senior English, which did not emphasize the
basic skills.

Teacher Responses to the Program

Teachers had three reactions to the program. First, it violated
their conceptions of appropriate teaching. Their specific
concerns varied according to their perspectives. The academic
teachers objected to the drill activities used to prepare students
for the minimum competency and district achievement tests.
These teachers referred to the drill activity as "teaching to the
test" to indicate that they did not view it as a legitimate form of
instruction.

We aren't teaching them how to think. We're teaching
them how to take tests. [10]

We're test oriented here. No teacher objects to that. Our emphasis is too much in some areas though. We spend so much time reviewing grammar in the eleventh and twelfth grade. There should be more reading and developing though processes and interpretation skills. Our children aren't being prepared for college in terms of what they read. [06]

Eight teachers raised this argument.

Teachers who took a balanced or vocational perspective disliked the requirement that they specify the date by which specific objectives would be reached. They were concerned that if a student did not master the objective in the required time, they would not have an opportunity to provide more assistance:

There shouldn't be as much emphasis on dates. Even if you get a week behind, the kids should master an objective. They're pushed and pushed and pushed. They've been pushed too far already. That's why they are where they are. [51]

I have a student who can't divide. How do you teach him volume and area? Is it better to teach division or to follow the objectives? [24]

Six teachers voiced this concern. They actually shared the administrations goal of teaching students basic skills. However, they were divided over the means, whether it was better to help students master specific objectives—sometimes including pre-requisite skills—or to touch on everything that would be tested. This division created friction:

I don't gear myself to the quarterly. I gear myself to the class. It doesn't matter to me if the date I'm supposed to finish is February 22 and I finish on February 28. If the administration wants to reprimand me, that's their prerogative, but I won't change. [05]

Teachers who did not teach basic skills per se resented having activities that focused on those topics added to their courses:

> We have to put basic skills into our lesson plans for each day. When you are teaching [a foreign language], you teach basic skills every minute, but you must write in a basic skills objective. Talk about paper work. I play the game, but isn't it silly? [14]

> I'd like to drop all the writing part from [my field]. Maybe allow more creativity. Students resent the time they spend reading and note taking. They get tense for that. It always happens just before an objective . . . Most of the learning comes from the hands-on not the written part. [56]

Teachers who used a great deal of hands-on activities objected to the scans. The coding procedures counted getting out materials and cleaning up as time off task. This policy reduced the instructional time scores in craft-oriented classes, and teachers feared those scores would give the impression that time was being wasted. They saw getting out materials as an integral part of the learning process or at least necessary for the craft activities and felt that their work was being misrepresented by the instructional time score. One teachers who was not as dependent upon activities with elaborate setup and cleanup tasks noted that she could do such activities, but she would make a point of not doing them when she was being scanned [14]. Six teachers mentioned this concern.

A second reaction to the program was that the formal accountability scheme reduced the complex, interactive aspect of teaching to numbers and checkpoints that were too simplistic to capture the intricacies of instruction. Teachers believed that much of their work required coping with contingencies they did not control, but the accountability scheme seemed to ignore those factors.

To teachers, the most important contingency was the students. This was apparent in their concerns about the scans when their instructional time scores were heavily dependent upon student performances. In some instances students could work for the teacher:

> [This class] is undisciplined, not physically. In terms of responsibility and concentration span. I had [a district official and an outsider] drop in. They were so good. They asked questions and gave answers. Afterwards, I asked them why they were so good. They said, "We wanted them to think we like you." That's the greatest accolade. [43]

A class could also work against a teacher. Another teacher told about a class that was so worried by the presence of the principal that students would not participate at all [51]. Teachers were also quite aware of how individual students responded to the scan process. One told about a student who figured out that the observer was counting the number of students looking down at each click of the clock. That student made a point of looking up and away everytime the clock clicked [21]. Another told of a student who pretended to study through an observation period because she did not know why the observer was there [53].

Students' unpredictability also affected teachers' ability to stay on the schedule specified in the QTP. Sometimes the issue was the students' ability to master the material: "In algebra, we did a unit on fractions and polymonial fractions. I thought it would be easy, but it wasn't so I lengthened that section. I've been able to cut days off of other topics" [26]. At other times the concern was student behavior: "If I'm supposed to do paragraphs, and one kid comes in and is gonna beat another kid up, you have to work on coping skills. Why are you gonna beat him up? Let's make a list of pros and cons. You can't deal with that with QTPS. You're not supposed to deviate. I do. The dates are not that worthwhile" [54]. It was not just that the forms could not account for such routine unexpected events. The administration of the supervisory system did not reflect what teachers saw as important:

> [My supervisor] came in unannounced. Two kids came in from the gym and one tried to pick a fight with the other.

I told them they couldn't fight here. I took them into the hall and calmed them down. Then I let them back in the class and conducted class . . . After class my supervisor told me my lesson plans and quarterlies didn't match like it's a big to-do . . . I don't care! It's the class that counts. [24]

Although students were the primary contingency, administrative action was another. Teachers did not know enough details of the administration of tests or assemblies to be able to accurately set dates for quarterlies.

It's nice to try to plan ten weeks in advance, but you can't plan for the minimum basic skills test or the achievement test or activity days ten weeks in advance. You can have the dates, but you won't know how it will impact on your courses. You can't find tune it that well. [01]

They expect us to use the quarterlies as weeklies. The weekly lesson plans are to be followed, but things change. Today some classes are thirty minutes long. Some are forty minutes and some are sixty minutes. Today's plans are shot. They'll say this situation is unique because of the testing, but there are three or four testing sessions a year. [06]

Between the students and administrators, twelve teachers believed that they could not predict events well enough to set a schedule in advance. As a result, they felt that they were being held accountable for events that were only partly under their control.

The third reaction was that the administration of the program violated teachers' conceptions of appropriate relationship with administrators. One manifestation of this concern was a recurring objection to the way teachers' time was used. Teachers objected that their time was "wasted" on things not directly related to their teaching work. This objective spread well beyond the improvement program itself to repeated complaints about the length of staff meetings. A related concern was the amount of paperwork teachers had to do. Eleven teachers stated this problem.

Within the program, concerns about time and paperwork focused on the QTPs. Teachers objected that the work put in on these and related documents did not contribute to their teaching:

> We don't do quarterlies for ourselves. We do them for the administration. [51]

> The quarterlies are redundant. Everything in the quarterlies is in the curriculum. I know where I'm going. I'd rather use the time to do things for the class. [The principal] says, "but you're given time to fill out the quarterlies." That's not the point. Why do things that are already done? [14]

> I was out sick one week last year. My plans were complete. I keep them on my desk like I'm supposed to though I don't need them. I called in after three days. The administrators didn't know what to do with my class. I said use my plans. They said the plans are not for the sub. They're for you. Well, Damn! I don't need the plans. [35]

Indeed, two teachers offered minor revisions in the three existing, but overlapping, forms—the curriculum, the QTPs, and the lesson plans—that would reduce paperwork teachers had to do. The administration's failure to make such changes was frustrating to teachers. One referred to this aspect of his job as "scribe work."

A more general reflection on teacher-administrator relations was what was described as a prevailing negativism.

> My attitude is things are getting better. They could get better still if some administrators would be kinder to teachers . . . Four or five years ago, the superintendent said, let's accentuate the positive. They accentuate the negative. [25]

I don't know if the perception of the administration is that teachers are lazy, inept, or incapable. We're treated with disdain, maybe with contempt. There's a very negative environment perpetuated by the administration. [09]

Sometimes a pat on the back helps more than a kick you know where. [48]

This negativism was detected in little actions. For instance, the math teacher who was reprimanded for not having lesson plans and QTPs that match after she had broken up a fight made the following comment: "[The supervisor's] tone of voice annoyed me like I was a bad kid. I'd better fix things up before they come to evaluate me or they'll put me on record" [24]. More frequently, teachers pointed to the accountability system as something that implied that all teachers were bad teachers:

This district says 10 percent of the people aren't doing their job so let's make everyone dot their i's and cross their t's and do ridiculous, rudimentary things to cover those 10 percent. [35]

I was told [the scans] were not intended for me. They were for the bad teachers. That's ridiculous. It's caused morale problems. People are antagonistic. [43]

There are a lot of good people here who are never told they're good. A lot of people who care, who are too professional to waste time in class. To have scans assumes that you may not be doing that. [41]

With such a formalized system, there might have been a concern that it was being used to punish and remove teachers. Opinion was divided on this question. Three teachers explicitly indicated that punishment was not a concern:

No one puts pressure on you to follow the quarterly. They're defeated because there are too many of us. How can one person monitor quarterlies and plans and be a disciplinarian?

Q: Can't they tell by observing?

No . . . You can write down something that makes sense to you but that others don't understand so they can't tell if you're doing it or not. [46]

Other people referred to incidents where procedures were being used to remove people:

[My evaluation] looked fair. It was better than average with these lousy evaluations they are giving now. [46]

They decide to nail one teacher . . . People who've been here twenty or thirty years suddenly get poor evaluations. You wonder how that can be after twenty years of no bad evaluations. [49]

To summarize, teachers did not see the program as something that helped them teach students better. Instead, they identified specific procedures that violated their conceptions of good teaching, they were worried about a system that seemed too rigid and simplistic to reflect the contingencies of teaching, and they believed that it was administered in a way that violated their conception of appropriate teacher-administration relationships.

The Program and Basic Skills Competence

Although the program contributed to the strained working conditions for teachers and to the tensions with administrators, it had its intended effects on student test scores. Between the springs of 1980 and 1985, the percentage of students passing the state minimum competency test increased from 53.9 to 93.9 in communications skills and from 36.8 to 88.6 in computation. This test was limited to ninth graders, but all students took the California Achievement Test (CAT) each spring. In the reading and mathematics results for all four grades in the high school between 1980 and 1985, there were forty possible changes in scores from one year to the next. Of these, twenty-six were increases, eight were declines, and six times there was no change. The average reading scores for all four grades increased 1.38 grade points in that five-year period. Mathematics scores increased 1.88 grade points during the same time. In 1985 the state removed the district's provisional certification and reduced the frequency of its monitoring of the district.

Although the program clearly succeeded in terms of the objectives set for it, teachers and administrators differed in their explanations for why it worked. The administrators tended to see the whole package of activities—including the scans, the QTPs, the test preparation activities, and the exhortation—as important, with a heavy emphasis on the first three. Teachers, especially those with the academic perspective, took a more narrow view:

> If you teach to the test, how can you go wrong. [08]

> I realize the kids did better on the tests. The reason is that for the last few years we've been more conscious of preparing for tests. Test besting. I can't see how else we're improving. [07]

From their perspective, some of the more intrusive aspects of the program—especially the scans and the quarterlies—did not contribute substantially to the improvement in test scores.

CONCLUSION

The Monroe High School story illustrates how a school's culture reflects main currents in national educational thought and some of the difficulties in applying those national ideas when they come into conflict with local conditions. It also suggests some lessons about the relationship between culture and additive change.

The four perspectives expressed by Monroe teachers— academic, balanced, vocational, and psychological development— responded to distinct populations that American high schools are expected to serve. None of these perspectives dominated locally, just as none of these populations dominate thinking about the comprehensive ideal. The combination of populations and options for them gives the comprehensive high school its egalitarian character. Equity if promoted by placing students in a situation with alternatives and letting each one choose a course of study. This system works because there is a fundamental acceptance of diversity (Powell, Farrar, and Cohen, 1985). This acceptance was well established in Monroe as part of an expectation that teachers would specialize. The idea of specialization was so taken for granted that it was rarely discussed, but it was so strongly held that it was taken as sacred. No one in the district could conceive of deviating from the departmental structure even when only a quarter of the high school's teachers were working on the superintendent's primary objective: basic skills improvement.

Maintaining the comprehensive ideal is difficult at schools like Monroe, where the student body does not meet the ideal's assumptions of diversity of achievement. Where students only reflect a limited part of the achievement distribution, they cannot take advantage of the fuller comprehensive menu. The misfit between the national ideal and the specific situation can create strains like the ones seen in Monroe.

This problem was manifest largely in teachers' definitions of those they included in the school's community. Inclusion is important because community members are treated as fellow humans and accorded a level of respect and concern that is not offered to the "outsider" (Schlechty, 1976). Teachers were most willing to admit students into the community who could help them pursue their own instructional purposes. Since these purposes varied according to one's perspective, some teachers were more inclusive than others. The most exclusive extreme was reached by the academic teachers, who would only include "real A students," a vanishing breed, in their opinion. Other students were belittled, not accorded the full benefit of those teachers' ability to explain concepts, and in some case pushed out of the classroom. These teachers continued to be unhappy that there were not enough of the "right kind" of students to allow them to achieve their instructional purposes. Academic specialization had a sacred quality to it; it was an anchor that defined their purpose for teaching. Thus, these teachers would not adjust their objectives to meet the needs of their students, and could not conceive of doing so. Teachers holding other perspectives were generally more inclusive and more satisfied with their work.

The consequences of exclusion can be severe. Cusick (1983) and Powell and colleagues (1985) have documented one consequence for students in the form of the "treaties" or "contracts" between teachers and students where grades are traded for compliant behavior. Examples of such treaties were apparent in Monroe, along with such behaviors as failing large numbers of students who did not meet the teacher's standards, diluting the curriculum, cryptic teaching, insulting students, and pushing them out of the classroom. Continuing interaction between teachers and students who "did not fit" within their community also took its psychic toll on teachers.

The comprehensive ideal is a major barrier to building agreement on a delimited set of instructional ends in a high school. Such a concentration runs counter to that ideal's fundamental commitment to diversity. Yet, there is evidence that concentration on basic skills instruction is effective in helping students learn minimum literacy skills (Clark, Lotto, and McCarthy, 1980; Wellisch et al., 1978). The Monroe story indicates that recommending a focused set of instructional ends is not just advocating a technique for instructional improvement; it raises fundamental questions of purpose. When effective schools researchers recommend focused attention to limited purposes, they do so in the name of a particular educational goal: guaranteeing minimal literacy skills to children of the urban poor that equal those of the middle class (Edmonds, 1979). This goal stems from a specific definition of equity based on comparable skills. When high school teachers resist this concentration of effort, they do so out of deep convictions that different instructional ends are important. They are firmly committed to teaching their specialties and to assumptions of diversity that allow them to continue doing so. These assumptions, although rarely articulated by teachers, are based on a different conception of equity: one based on student choice. In effect, the specialist teachers at Monroe used different criteria for effectiveness than those proposed by effective schools researchers.

Still, the minimum skills definition of equity is another important current in American educational thought. In the Monroe setting it was not reflected in the teacher culture so much as in the state's minimum competency test and in the commitments of district administrators. Although these commitments were reinforced by the state test, it would be a mistake to read them as just a cynical effort to cope with external pressure. The administrators' commitment was sincere, although they did not always understand the tensions between the comprehensive ideal and the minimum skills objective. That may be why they accepted an additive approach to change that did not encompass cultural transformation; they were willing for behavior to change even if attitudes did not.

The Monroe improvement program was a success in its own terms. Test scores clearly rose. Students learned more and performed better even if they did not yet meet the standards set by the academic teachers. This measurable improvement is a considerable accomplishment.

At one level the program succeeded because it did not intend to create cultural change. It did not seek to build consensus on the importance of basic skills instruction, nor did it try to convince teachers to develop expectations that all students could learn. Instead, it enforced specified formal arrangements and behaviors. Its centerpiece was the monitoring procedure that verified that those arrangements and behaviors were in place. The curriculum alignment work and test preparation activity insured that time was devoted to instruction on what would be tested. The strategy circumvented teachers' beliefs and relied upon formal authority. Although teachers were allowed to participate to a certain extent, especially in the design of the curriculum, the fundamental elements of the program were centrally mandated, and the formal evaluation system was used to inforce them. Teachers had little choice about accepting administrative directives on how time should be spent. Thus, one of the most important lessons from Monroe High School is that centrally enforced behavioral change can be implemented and have its desired effect even if it runs counter to teachers' sacred beliefs.

But change came with a cost. Although the success of the Monroe improvement program was notable, it did not touch some crucial issues at all. The significant proportion of teachers who would not admit most students into the school community did not change their views. Cryptic teaching, insulting students, and pushing the worst ones out of the class continued. Moreover, the blatant use of authority was widely resented by more teachers than those who wanted to teach "better" students. Because of it, teachers came to exclude administrators from the school community just as many of them excluded most students. In fact, the exclusion of administrators was substantially more universal. Tensions surrounding the change program contributed to the formation of a culture of opposition among teachers. The roots of this culture preceded the project, but project implementation contributed to it substantially. This conflict created a situation in which teachers complied with the letter of those parts of the program that were monitored, but not its spirit. In fact, wherever they could, they continued to operate as they had before the project. The project also added to the sense of stress and discomfort of teachers who worked at Monroe. As such, it was a major contributor to teachers' burnout and eagerness to leave.

In sum, although the program reached its stated objectives, it did so by ignoring some problems stemming from the teachers' culture and exacerbating others. It could safely be predicted that the program would only continue as long as strong administrators at the top of the district were willing to enforce it.

3

Westtown: Improvement Efforts in a Good School

Norms about teaching, administrative behavior, and how a school should operate vary in the degree to which staff members are willing to consider adopting alternatives to them. Some expectations for behavior are grounded in "the state of the art" and are followed as long as experience, research and common sense provide no contradictory guidance; other norms are based more on legalistic considerations and change only in so far as developments in legislatures and the courts warrant; still another set of norms is rooted primarily in moral issues—that is, determinations of what is good that tend to define purpose and establish order in one's world—and these show a remarkable resilience, as the adherence to teaching one's specialty did at Monroe.

This book argues that norms that lie at the core of one's professional identity can take on sacredlike qualities. At Westtown, teachers revered the instructional process in the classroom. Who made decisions affecting the classroom, how they were made, and the content of the decisions were much less important than whether the process and the products of such decision making implicated the quality of classroom activity and the type of relationship among teachers and students needed to make the activity worthwhile. In other words, the teachers were not interested in preserving professional autonomy as much as they were adamant about not comprising the quality of instruction. The reason for teaching, for most Westtown teachers, was inseparably tied to this norm. Working under alternatives to this expectation was inconceivable. Indeed, guidance from this case suggests that a plausible test of whether the sacred is being tampered with is a prevailing desire to remove oneself, either psyshically or actually, from the setting. The metaphor of the sacred, then, captures an essential quality of the normative structure of Westtown, and much of the case is devoted to detailing this notion.

Events at Westtown also highlight two additional points about the relationship between a school's culture and change. First, initiatives that threaten sacred norms are greeted with more than planned stubbornness or thoughtful resistance. Because the sacred establishes order, challenges strike deeply. As a result, staff members experience emotional, physical, and mental consequences, and often begin seriously questioning their efficacy and that of others.

Second, the case cautions that not all school improvement efforts involve cultural change. Change can be primarily technical and/or political as well, as several authors have noted (House, 1981; Tichy, 1983; Corbett and Rossman, 1986). Cultural change results from normative challenges. At Westtown, curriculum development and instructional improvement activities were not at odds with existing concepts of appropriate classroom or administrative behavior. Incorporating new ideas learned during these activities was free of traumas. On the other hand, changes in the disciplinary system violated the sacredness of the instructional process and met dramatic responses.

This chapter, after presenting background information on Westtown, begins with staff reactions to recent changes in the school and contrasts these to the faculty's historical assessment of the place. It then describes the essential tenets of the school's culture and details the interaction between it and three sets of school improvement activities.

WESTTOWN HIGH SCHOOL

This is a whole push toward academic excellence. [87]

We have good teachers. They're doing it. They hate it. But

if we can get through the tension in this transformation, we will have a great school. [1]

Change is difficult. Whether it involves reordering social relationships in a society or improving instructional practices in a school, the alteration of behavior is typically accompanied by questioning and concern. This is no less the case in good schools trying to become better than in mediocre schools trying to become good.

By all accounts, Westtown was a "good" school—whether from the perspective of its staff, the community, educators in the region, or formal accrediting agencies. Yet, this medium-sized suburban school (just over one thousand students in grades seven through twelve) had not completely escaped the problems attendant with a changing student population (in terms of numbers and academic ambition) and slowly eroding standardized test scores. The consequence was a systematic administrative push to improve academic excellence, signaled by the arrival of a new principal.

Motivated partially by a desire to "recapture" an instructional reputation that attracted homebuyers to the community and to maintain favorable comparisons with surrounding school districts that served wealthier families, the administration instituted multiple changes affecting the curriculum, teaching practices, accountability, and discipline. The curriculum was altered to offer more challenging "advanced placement" courses to academically talented youngsters, to revamp the overall scope and sequence in several academic departments, and to upgrade at least two other departments to enable them to be at the forefront of instruction in their fields. Changes in teaching practices were encouraged through a series of Madeline Hunter workshops led by an assistant principal in the building. Increased accountability for student learning was promoted by instituting departmentwide mid-term examinations, increasing teacher analyses and reporting of test results, and increasing administrative reliance on standardized test scores as evidence of instructional quality. A change in the system of handling discipline problems was earmarked by the instituting of a point system whereby specific consequences would result from a student's accumulation of a certain number of points.

Teachers reacted differently to the various initiatives. Changes related to curriculum and instruction, on the whole, won wide acceptance. Accountability changes generated more complaints but received a reluctant compliance. On the other hand, the discipline efforts sparked hostility and more than an occasional refusal to comply. Examining the differences in responses reveals much about the school's culture—not only about the component norms, beliefs, and values concerning the appropriate definitions of a good school, but also about the intensity with which those cultural elements were held.

THE FACULTY TALKS

Teachers' comments about working at Westtown and recent events revealed a Januslike quality. Occasionally they would almost laugh and cry at the same time. Sadness attended portrayals of recent events; happiness accompanied descriptions of the school's proud tradition. This section carries the reader first into a widespread despair shared by most teachers concerning the school's immediate future. It then steps back and lets the very same staff members present the other side of the coin.

It's pretty much like the New Deal . . . .When they're changing things too much, you get the feeling they don't know what they're doing. [6]

I have some inkling of a belief that people are not seeing where leadership is taking us. [10]

What teachers desperately need is to know that someone out there knows what they're doing. [11]

No one knows where we're going. People say we're just changing to change. [27]

The faculty doesn't feel like it's going anywhere . . . It stems from the changes. They don't see what we have accomplished. [33]

Kids don't know where we're going. All the changes in rules and regulations, they don't know what they are. The teachers are in the same situation. You don't know where you stand; whether you make the right decision, whether rules will be adhered to, or whether your program is viewed positively. [34]

There has been a series of changes; so it can be confusing. [46]

The school is in a state of stress . . . so many changes and alterations to the changes. That's difficult to cope with in any setting. [55]

I'm not sure what the rules are. Instead of there being an accepted pattern, people aren't sure. [69]

An unsettled feeling drifted through the faculty. Teachers shared a sense that they did not know "what is" in the school. Immersed in a changing situation, they had no fixed point by which to assess direction. The faculty's tone recalled Benjamin Franklin's observation at the conclusion of the constitutional convention that until that point he had been unable to determine whether the sun on the back of Washington's chair was rising or setting, but now—considering the quality of the group's work—he believed the sun to be rising. Time had not yet made the resolution of events at Westtown clear to the teachers, although those that hazarded a prediction suggested a setting sun:

It appears to be changing for the sake of changing. When I came to the school, some instructional change was taking place; [but] you could cite the reason for it. It was obvious. It seems like [now] we're in a roll with no end in sight. [5]

On paper, everything changes; nothing ever changes really. [79]

There is constant change and constant interference and not for the better. People are not petty; they are willing to change for the better. [8]

The changes haven't all been for the better. Sure, every school needs to improve, but sometimes [the change] is so drastic that it affects everybody. You hear so much complaining. It's a morale factor, like a disease. [15]

The big thing I've gotten is that things are not going in a positive direction. [18]

This was a nice place. [23]

I don't know if it ever peaked or just stayed on an even plane, but in that last three years, it's gone down. [28]

What we're afraid of is that the school will soon lose that [good] reputation. [35]

Results aren't showing us to be better. There's only more confusion. [44]

We went from the top of the hill to this giant mudslide . . . At best we're staying even. The school is going around in circles. [47]

I see too many changes and the staff's morale going down. [58]

The uncertainty and despair for the future revealed in these statements had several precipitates: actually leaving the school or a desire to do so, mental and physical health problems, and increasing apathy. By themselves, these reactions were dramatic enough and demanding of an outsider's attention. However, they also served as the closest indicators available that sacred norms were being implicated in some way. When faced with the possibility of a sacredlike norm's diminution, the immediate response was to express a desire to leave the situation, either actually or psychically or both. An inability to do so had serious emotional consequences.

By the beginning of the 1985–86 school year, actual turnover was less than statements made the previous spring would have indicated would be the case. Only two teachers actually left voluntarily. Although one of these had said a lateral move was as attractive as an upward one, the new position was in fact a step up. On the other hand, all of the people seeking employment elsewhere were veteran teachers with relatively high salaries. The folklore—and probably the fact—is that school districts do not readily hire people they will have to pay highly, and this reality may have inhibited the veterans from leaving. As staff members talked, substantial anguish accompanied their consideration of even changing jobs. For example:

I want to get into something where I'm not beaten down. [67]

I applied to [another district]. I took it as a compliment that I got to the final interview round. But I figured they'd not want to pay my salary. [10]

Five years ago I would have said I'm delighted to be staying. Now, the answer is unfortunately yes. I have applied other places. I don't want to be this disgruntled for ten [more] years. [15]

I would prefer to leave now. [19]

I've considered getting out. [29]

I'm thinking of early retirement. I hadn't thought about it until this year. Sometimes I wish I had done something else with my life. [52]

I have an interview on Thursday. [28]

The situation is pushing some people into speeding up their search, expediting it. If I could get social security, I'd retire. [34]

And the rumors of people leaving exacerbated a sense of potentially dramatic turnover:

You hear all the time that somebody's leaving. You don't know who. [16]

The majority of staff would have left last spring, laterally. [But] too many have no place to go; they are too high up the ladders. So they will turn their heads, walk into the room, and do what they have to do to get by. I'm almost in that category. I'm looking. [47]

The teachers who were considering leaving were not just concentrated among the oldest staff. Although six of the above had more than twenty years of experience in the school, teachers who wanted to leave included those who had been in Westtown for longer and shorter periods than the average (12.4 years for the seventy-one from whom information on their years in the school was available). Moreover, the teachers talking about leaving and the ones who left were not impossibly intractable or deadwood in the eyes of their colleagues. Indeed, one of the major fears, real or imagined, that turnover produced was that good people would continue to leave, robbing the school of its heart.

My fear is that the changes would make us lose good people. We have lost some but they were close to retirement anyway. [19]

People are afraid that people will get disgusted and leave. [20]

I'm concerned, and the people they bring in may not be as good as the ones that leave. [26]

It's taken a lot of the spirit out of the good ones. [54]

Health problems, too, emerged. A few staff members claimed physical ailments; even more described a decline in what could be labeled "mental health." Assuming that a major component of this health was having positive and constructive thoughts about one's work place, the following statements support an argument for such a decline:

I've never despised coming to work. In the last month, I'm thinking about it. [7]

The attitude is changing. Before I couldn't wait to get up and come. [11]

We have a lot of unhappy people in school. You hear so much complaining. It's a morale factor, like a disease . . . It used to be nice here. [15]

This is my worst year in education other than the first . . . I have a friend [on the faculty] who can't sleep on Sundays. [52]

There is a lot of unrest and unhappiness. [86]

I see a lot of unhappy people. [3]

I used to thoroughly enjoy coming here. [29]

The last three to five years I felt it. Before that, I never went home and complained. [30]

When I leave here, I don't want to think about the place. [33]

Teachers are weary and disgruntled. It's depressing. [36]

I used to love getting up to come here. Now I'm looking to change, even laterally. [37]

I'm being treated for anxiety. [26]

At one point last year, I was throwing up every morning before I came. [21]

Several teachers are on Valium, pressure-relieving drugs. Maybe I should be too. [28]

Teachers are dissatisfied, frustrated, misunderstood, and short-changed. [41]

Staff members offered the above comments with a significant amount of emotion. But what follows came with the most noticeable accompaniment of shrugs, grimaces, and wistful stares. For teachers the most tell-tale sign of what they perceived to be the deterioration of the school were apathy and withdrawal. Illustrative comments include the following:

A number of people have fled, retired early, or come in when they are supposed to, do competent jobs and go on. [5]

People loved to teach here. Now they're saying I'll just put in my time. [8]

It's a tough atmosphere to work in . . . I hope people don't get so down so they just come in, teach, and leave. [12]

I'm seeing some people let some things go. [53]

There's a lot of good teachers who have just given up . . . It's rotting from within . . . It's a crime . . . A lot of teachers are playing out their string. [22]

Since then, people said to hell with it. I'll just go in to my room and close the door. I'm going solo, do my thing. [16]

Teachers also noticed that their colleagues were not going out of their way to participate in the extracurricular life of the school:

I used to be very involved in things. Now I still coach, but that's all. It used to be you didn't have to beg people to come chaperone. Now it comes to Friday and you have to beg. It didn't used to be that way. People used to volunteer. People are tired of not getting anything back for it. [20]

We have a faculty that would go above and beyond. People would do these things without thinking about it. Now they do things as if it were personally a burden. [58]

Look into absenteeism, people are giving up activities. [23]

So teachers are saying, I will do the job in the classroom. But it doesn't make for the kind of school we want. People volunteered to do jobs; now they don't want any of them— chaperones, advisors. It's not a matter of not wanting to deal with kids but everything else has shut them down. [35]

Frustration and sadness were evident in the comments. Three spoke for the majority of the faculty:

With the changes coming on, you can almost see why people become deadwood. [29]

In the long run, kids will suffer. We'll just turn into average teachers. I'll leave before I do that. [37]

It's so much different. We still laugh but it's not a laugh of humor; it's a laugh of sadness. Like in the service, when all hell was breaking loose. [6]

Teachers' comments about Westtown were particularly poignant. Their number reflected the extent of their feelings. Of the eighty-four teachers interviewed, the comments of forty are represented in the above quotes; at least twenty-six others echoed similar personal concerns about school direction and staff attitudes. Indeed, most telling is that out of the teachers interviewed, only seven or eight acknowledged that they still looked forward to arriving at the school each day.

The Other Side of the Coin

Perhaps teachers everywhere in any school reflect this degree of disgruntlement with their work life. A Harris survey in 1985 indicated that 27 percent of teachers nationwide were ready to leave their jobs (Kanengiser, 1985). It is doubtful, however, that teachers everywhere could, almost in the same breath, make the following statements about their schools, colleagues, or programs:

The amount of learning going on this school is tremendous. [78]

The quality that comes out [of this program], you could put it up with any school. [40]

It's a good school statewide. [60]

Academically, it's a fine school. [71]

I think it's a great place. [44]

The school used to be a very well-respected school. We have the tradition [that keeps people going]. I teach for the kids. [22]

This a good school. I love it. I fight for it tooth and nail. [26]

I still have pride in [the school]. We know how great we were. [47]

I came here because I was so impressed with it. [58]

We always felt confident in the classroom. The staff built this reputation. We've worked hard for it. It was built up on consistency and discipline. [37]

Staff members believed that much of what was good about the school was attributable to the quality of the teachers and how they approached their work.

The good news is that the faculty is marvelous—giving, concerned, wonderful to work with. That's what made this school great. [11]

I found the faculty to be very cooperative. I enjoy talking to them in informal situations. The faculty is warm, good to me, very helpful. I've gotten cooperation on the times I ask about materials, just to get ideas. [18]

I am amazed at the [positive] feeling among the faculty. It has been present the whole time. If anything, maybe we've gotten a little closer. [74]

There are no better people to work for. [82]

This is an unusual faculty. The main core is an unusually good group of people. We know we have this reputation. As a homeowner, I can see it in terms of property values. People moved in. Now I see people moving out because of the school. What is carrying the faculty, they still have pride. They don't want to see this bad reputation. Maybe subconsciously they're fighting. [16]

We're a real friendly group. When I came, people couldn't

do enough to help me . . . even the subs say they get more help here than anyplace else. [23]

Through sincerity, perseverance, know-how, enthusiasm—we're cultivating a sense of unity and purpose in the other [department] members. We have excellent rapport. Each recognizes the others' skills and professionalism. [25]

The finest group of teachers I've ever known. I marvel at them. [26]

The faculty and administration are very warm, very helpful. If they saw other schools, they would realize this is a good place. [51]

Our department is one of the outstanding [in the area]—very professional [29]

Our program is excellent. Why? Basically we're a bunch that wants to do a good job. They're workers. We make our system work. We disagree violently on many things; but in the long run, we're working for the same thing. [34]

The only reason our department is successful is the dedicated staff. [42]

We are close knit. We protect one another. If one person is affected, we are all affected. We are forerunners. [49]

A number of people have been here a long time; they prided themselves on the quality of the program. They've always been trend-setters. [54]

These data portray an almost schizophrenic faculty. Teachers presented themselves as a faculty in turmoil, questioning the school's direction and effectiveness, and yet they claimed devotion to one another and to seeing to it that students learned. To better understand what was going on in the school, it is imperative to delineate three major tenets of the school's professional ethos.

WESTTOWN'S ETHOS

The tenets of the high school's professional ethos evolved slowly. Earmarked by remarkable stability during the 1970s in terms of low teacher and administrator turnover, the school offered a fertile environment for a strong normative system to take root. This is exactly what happened. Facing few external challenges, staff members were able to focus almost exclusively on the business of teaching students. Benefitting from frequent interaction with one another and insulation from other influences, the staff developed strong commitments to how this work should be conducted. Three interrelated sets of expectations formed the foundation of this system. First, as one teacher stated it, "the classroom is the capitol," a phrase that pointed to the area of central concern for the teachers. The next two sets, profane in nature, derived from the first: discipline should be consistent, and the principal should protect the school from the outside world.

The Classroom is the Capitol

One administrator's formula for making a school good was straightforward: "You get good people, let them go and keep them happy" [3]. Teachers adamantly agreed. Their job was to teach students, plain and simple. However, they did not reject input as to how that job could be done better, nor did they seek to work in isolation from their colleagues. To the contrary, supervision was usually welcomed, and staff members demonstrated a resoluteness in updating curriculum offerings. Indeed, in recent years, at least five departments undertook revisions affecting all reachers, and another four adjusted course offerings. Of course, one might accuse the faculty of just going with the times, and there is a delicate balance between trying to be relevant and appearing to be trendy. Nevertheless, a sincere willingness to take risks in order to improve instruction lay behind the actions.

> Curriculum changes I don't mind. I've always used my own method. Now I'm incorporating more department stuff. I don't like it, but I see the positive. It gets you out, maybe you were in a rut. It stimulates you. [7]

We've changed around the curriculum. It hasn't been all that upsetting. It sort of brought order to a situation that was upsetting. Back in the sixties, it was do your own thing, ended up with thirty-five to thirty-six different courses. You name it, we had it. Now, it's more structured, and just what we needed. [4]

When I first came, we had a nice program, a well-structured combination of electives and required courses. Two years later we got the idea of the grab-bag thing. The students could take any course. It was a time of the fads. It seems like we're getting it back. There was constant realigning, constant new this, that and the other. Now there is more continuity and stability—except now we have to revise the syllabus and develop an overview [of a new course]. [6]

I'm excited about what we're going to work on. We could be the first in the state to do it. That's kind of neat. A lot of it is due to the faculty that's here. [53]

In eight years, my department has gone through two revisions and three systems. It's a lot of work. I like the system we have now. [70]

Every school needs to improve. [15]

[A teacher] and I have been working together, seeing why there was a difference [in results of classroom activities]. If I do something that went well, I tell [the other teacher]. [31]

The result was that the faculty took joyous pride in the products of their efforts. Adding to the comments presented at the end of the first section of this chapter were two more:

We have the best equipment [in this region]. Our program is a Cadillac; I'm very proud of it. [27]

I think our program is excellent. [34]

The driving force behind the teachers' curriculum

improvement activities seemed to be to provide the very best instruction they could in the classroom. The following comments reflect an attitude not only expressed throughout the interviews but also evidenced in actual teaching.

I teach for the kids. [22]

What holds a marriage together is commitment. That commitment to be professional or serve children should hold a school. If held, despite the undertones, then it would be a compliment to the faculty. [10]

I'm here to do a job. I don't let the outside affect me. I close it out. [36]

We focus on what will work in the classroom . . . The rules here don't intrude on this. [84]

I want to promote the positive, to give kids something more that they can hold on to in the rest of their lives. [51]

I do more than required in my classroom. [52]

So many of the teachers respect education so much they will do whatever it takes to keep it going. [54]

You want to make sure you do your job so the next teacher can do theirs. [77]

Essentially this tenet of the cultural system specified that classroom decisions would be made on the basis of what was likely to insure the best instruction possible and not because of political or demographic considerations. Who made the decisions seemed less important than the criteria upon which the decision was based. Teaching to tests, caving in to parental demands, or lowering standards to help a less able student body succeed was anathema, as will be seen. A teacher summarized this attitude best: "There was a time when the classroom was the capitol; the administration existed to serve the teacher performing in an excellent manner—everything was done with learning as the ultimate goal" [25]. Thus, the classroom as the capitol evoked the idea that the classroom was the focal point of school life, the location of the most revered activities.

Discipline Should be Consistent

If one counted the words that occurred most frequently in teacher comments about how to treat students or teachers, *consistent*—closely followed by *follow through, backed up,* or *supported*—would have been at the top of the list. Of the eighty-four teachers interviewed, fifty-six used these very words. Should a discipline problem emerge, teachers wanted the student to be dealt with quickly and fairly, with the same criteria for making a judgment applied in every case. For them, this fairness made the school world predictable; the consequences of an action were known by all even before the action was committed. And as importantly, teachers' authority in the classroom was reinforced.

Make a rule and stick to it. [16]

We have policy; it's only as good as it is enforced. [29]

Discipline, when it's made up, applies to everyone. That's how I function as a teacher and have never had a problem with it. [30]

The plane leaves at 2:05. If you are not there, the plane leaves. [32]

You have to have a consistency in administering policies, to both faculty and students. [Otherwise] the faculty becomes aware if they don't do anything, no one will come down on them either, like the kids. [35]

I have no gripe with policies, if they are administered fairly. [37]

My philosophy is firm, fair, and consistent. Although I probably have the loosest atmosphere, at the same time they know what's expected. If they step out of line, they know they'll pay the price. [47]

If you make a rule, follow it through. [60]

It's not a question of what rules there are but how you handle them. [53]

Enforcement is the issue more than the policy. Why have policy you don't enforce? Consistency is the thing. [41]

Teachers felt that a serious problem would result if rules were not enforced consistently. And that was that students — and teachers — would no longer respond positively to the exercise of authority and thus would begin to behave as disruptively as they wished.

If you are going to have a rule, stick to it. With a lack of consistency, we lose our ability to be the authority. [8]

I got used to a set of rules, followed to a 'T.' It made for a well-run school. Kids have even said to me, "See what happens when students are not punished" . . . when you send a kid down for discipline and nothing happens, you feel like a jerk. [23]

When you run into a problem, you want something done about it right away. If the kid goes down and is told, "don't do that it's not nice," it breeds a lack of respect. They feel they can get away with it even when sent down to the office. [38]

Teachers also valued consistent discipline because they believed that it enabled them to devote all of their class time to instruction. Disruptive behavior was seen as another interference that took away from that time. One teachers summed up the feeling this way: "The faculty is concerned about discipline problems outside the classrooms and afraid that they will get into the class." [69].

However, teachers did not value passive students. Boisterous, enthusiastic, energetic, and even somewhat unruly behavior was tolerated and even desired by a majority of the faculty *if* that behavior was directed toward learning. One teacher, in fact, severely reprimanded the students one day for not being lively enough when a researcher was present in the class. The students explained they were afraid they would make the teacher look bad in front of an outsider, fearing the person would mistake their eager involvement in the discussion for a teacher's lack of control. At least five other teachers made a similar comment when their classes were observed, and at the same time bemoaned that the outsider had not seen the kids at their "best." As one teacher said, "You have to realize it's an artificial situation; the kids want to look good and make the teacher look good" [8].

Teachers, then, desired active participants in the classroom process. When students skipped out of line, swift and predictable but not necessarily harsh retribution was expected and demanded in order to preserve their classrooms for instruction.

The Principal Should Protect the School from the Outside

People often learn about themselves in retrospect. Or, as the aphorism goes, "You don't know what you've got until you lose it." Had the teachers been asked in 1980 what kind of administrative behavior they valued, they would have immediately discussed what a disciplinarian should do. If pushed to define desirable principal behaviors, the teachers would in all probability have been at a loss. To hear them talk, they had no idea what the principal in office at that time did. The principal was rarely seen in the halls, much less observed carrying out the duties of the office. Indeed, at the principal's retirement roast in 1982, a teacher stood up, introduced himself as a sophomore in the high school, and asked "Who is Mr. _____?" However, teachers subsequently began to value the activities that apparently went on behind the scenes.

> In the past, we never heard three-fourths of the silliness. I never realized it until the change. We were shielded. It's not being done now. We're no longer shielded from this kook or that kook. [8]

> With the other principal, we never saw [the person]. As it turns out, [the person] was doing a fantastic job of

buffering the faculty. But there was no real leadership. [16]

[The principal] stayed to himself. But things got done. People didn't realize it until he left. [32]

[The principal] kept a low profile but I didn't realize how good a job he did. He was a buffer between us and [the outside world]. [35]

The previous administration acted like a sponge. If we didn't need to know something, we didn't [learn about it]. A school needs a buffer. [47]

I always thought of an administrator as a mediator between the board and the teachers. [52]

Once again, it seems what teachers were really saying is that they wanted to be left to do their job. They did not recognize that administrative behavior played a part in maintaining the classroom as their province—other than to handle disruptive students—until the school and the community began to change.

The Tenets and the Sacred

Of the three tenets just discussed, the idea of the classroom as capitol approached the sacred. Staff members were unable to consider, much less approve of, decisions made on the basis of criteria (such as public relations, legalities, or political considerations) other than those related to improving learning; and at the heart of being a teacher at Westtown was the expectation that one's professional purpose was to provide the best instruction possible. Thus, this norm was central to professional identify, and deviance from it was more than distasteful—it was inconceivable that staff members holding this norm would be able to work under alternative expectations with satisfaction.

On the other hand, staff members acknowledged the existence of alternative administrative approaches to discipline. They felt that the alternatives were not preferable. The third tenet—the principal as buffer—was highly valued as well, but again, alternative forms of administration were recognized and not rejected out of hand in principle. The power that the latter two norms had for staff members derived solely from their relationship to preventing the classroom as the province of learning. And over time the regular occurrence of behaviors related to consistent discipline and administrative buffering symbolically affirmed their construction of professional reality.

CHANGE AT WESTTOWN

It is not quite accurate to say that all the changes that teachers thought they were facing were initiated with the arrival of a new principal. Curriculum change or revision was almost routine as teachers in various departments updated, increased the relevance of, or fine-tuned their offerings. In addition, and more importantly, if the majority of teachers were accurate in their assessment, the student body changed over time. Fewer college bound and academically oriented students dotted the classrooms; instead, according to teachers, a more apathetic, "me-oriented" clientele became prevalent. The following comments echo the thoughts of at least twenty-nine faculty members.

> Before, the attitude of kids was much better . . . kids are more complacent; it's harder to motivate them. [7]

> Kids don't have the same attitude. [13]

> I still feel the personality of the students has changed. It gnaws at people. It was happening before [the new principal] got here. [16]

> Are we different? Are we getting a lower-quality kid? I'm not any easier. But kids don't care as much. [23]

> I've got a second-period class. The kids are real nice, polite, courteous, and respectful; but they are not motivated. [28]

Before, young people adhered to rules and regulations. Now they question them. Standards I've used for years, I've had to alter them. Students are more blasé. [27]

Children today are a much more me-oriented group. I don't get the dedication. Very few kids are concerned about what you think. I'm seeing it much more. It's not all kids. [33]

Kids are not the same. You have a minority that is decent. [36]

Today there is a complete reversal. Materials are never taken home. Everything is too much trouble. They say, "You entertain me." [42]

There were only six clearly dissenting opinions; three were as follows:

Kids are kids. They have to be taught decision-making skills. Some people around find it convenient as an excuse. I don't change my classroom standards. I don't feel I have to change. [37]

You spell out what is expected. If kids know expectations, and they are carried out, [everything is fine]. We're not here to win friends; we're here to teach. [30]

I set my goals and stay after them. It's hard to work, [but] kids did the same things they do now. I want them to learn to be responsible. [24]

The point is that a potential challenge to the faculty's view of the school and how it should operate was already appearing on the scene. In this case, it coincided with an administrative change, one that from all indications was expected by the superintendent to instigate a number of improvement efforts. Faculty reactions to these changes illustrate the interplay between a professional culture and innovations. At Westtown, the reaction varied in the extent to which the change was congruent with the norm of the classroom as the capitol. Three of the changes over the last three years in particular are informative. (Other changes were made, including moving all special education students into regular classes, but these received less comment from teachers.)

Madeline Hunter

The Madeline Hunter approach to instruction is probably the most widely used instructional innovation in the country at the moment. Its appeal resides largely in its common sense, but research seems to bear out the enthusiasm for it (Stallings, 1985). In any case, it was readily accepted by one of the administrators at the high school. Convincing the superintendent of the worthiness of the program, the administrator and a cadre of other staff members attended training sessions. The sessions proved disappointing, but the administrator essentially went through the materials individually and developed a series of workshops to be given to the entire faculty over the course of a fall. The workshops were taught by that person, who intentionally and conscientiously modeled the desired behaviors while instructing the staff. Teachers were then to try out the ideas in their classrooms voluntarily for the remainder of the year, receiving commendations from administrators on evaluations if they were observed to be attempting some of the suggested practices. The following year evaluations would be based formally on adherence to the Hunter program.

Teacher reactions varied from neutral to extremely positive, with the majority being on the positive end. There was no discernible negative reactions.

Two trains of thought on Madeline Hunter: Some thought it was a waste of time, but for most, it was a rejuvenating experience. We were doing those things anyway but lost sight of the reason why. [8]

I have been using Madeline Hunter to the best I can. Sometimes it works, sometimes it doesn't. I try to use anticipatory set always, and I try to remember to erase the blackboard. [10]

Madeline Hunter went over well. I was pleasantly surprised. A lot of people used those techniques anyway. Maybe she isn't a guru, but they're doing it anyway. I didn't realize what I was doing. I have to admit that phrase "anticipatory set" goes through my mind. [12]

Madeline Hunter, I think, emphasizes to make each student accountable so I try to get work back [as soon as possible]. [14]

A lot of it is useful. It's probably the best workshop in a long time. Some of the techniques, I realized I should do more of them. [23]

The most valuable in-service I've been in. Fantastic. [29]

It was one of those rare times when we talked about what teaching really is. [80]

A lot of time was devoted to it. The points were excellent. There are things you do and find you've done it and now know why. It could have been condensed. [31]

Basically, teachers accepted the suggested practices as additional input into how to teach students better. The prospect of evaluation was not a resented imposition; instead, it was in line with a concern for making the classroom the locus of the most education the school could offer.

Accountability

The seeds for an increasing emphasis on grades and test scores were sown in 1976 when an outside evaluation team warned the school that, despite its excellence, it was in danger of becoming complacent. This event was recalled by both the superintendent and the new principal as a stimulus for introducing departmental midterm exams, regular grade reports by teachers, grade analyses by departmental chairpersons, and heightened reliance on standardized test scores and student scholarship awards as indicators of program quality. One of them commented, "I believe this happened: there was no accountability system; no one applied systems to see if the kids were learning."

Faculty members had mixed reactions to the changes. Most obvious to teachers was that accountability-related moves generated additional work. Just becoming more busy was a cause for complaints but not resistance, unless it came at the expense of planning for or handling classroom-related activities. For the most part, however, teachers complied and agreed with a greater emphasis on knowing where students stood.

> The standardized exams forced us to talk with each other to make sure the material is covered. [83]

> I work harder now, with attendance sheets, grade summaries, things of that nature, lesson plans to department chairpersons. [7]

> Like getting a test back the next day . . . If you don't, they're after you. You're working at night all the time. Then they throw other stuff on top of you. [4]

> Yesterday they turned the day around to accommodate tests. Instead of getting my break, I went all the way through. You talk about exhausted. It's just a lot of little things like that. We weren't giving as many tests, so there's a new emphasis to have some kind of indication of how kids are doing. I check them out all year so why all of a sudden this thing. [15]

> I don't have the time. Before I could pace myself. There is so much extra stuff now. I'm forced to lower my standards. For my own survival. [26]

> I work harder in the classroom; I have to demand more. [30]

> There is an enormous amount of paperwork. [36]

> My pet gripe is the paperwork. It seems to be more and more. [53]

> There is more paperwork. [39–and echoed by 38]

> The extra amount of paperwork is taking too much time [50]

> I feel I'm overworked. I can't give attention to one thing without feeling like I'm taking away from another. [40]

For a core of seven or eight teachers, the accountability to move was more sinister. Instead of improving instruction, the changes weakened it; instead of increasing student achievement, the changes forced teachers to deemphasize the aspects of their subjects they deemed to be of the most enduring value; and instead of raising standards, the changes in fact required teachers to lower them. The increased resentment seemed not so much related to a perceived outside intrusion into teacher classroom decisions as to a feeling that decisions affecting the classroom were not made with learning in mind. One teacher succinctly summarized the dilemma this collection of teachers perceived: "Students may show up as testing better, but it's done something to the whole emotional atmosphere. I will not do it wrong, but I don't want to hurt the kids on the midterm either . . . But a lot of what we're emphasizing is forgettable, except to teachers" [54].

The Disciplinary System

Administrators (with faculty committee input) implemented a point system for handling discipline. The stated purpose was "to separate academics from discipline," according to an administrator, by attaching specific consequences to the accumulation of particular point levels and, thereby, freeing the teachers from having to make judgments that could affect their instructional effectiveness. But these specific changes in the disciplinary system were not as important as the philosophy that teachers felt was behind the system or the manner in which that philosophy led the system to be enforced in reality.

> When the new leaders came together, they appeared to have a difficult philosophy. It has slowly emerged and added to already occurring changes. [5]

Before there was a consistency in how people were treated as far as discipline. [Now] each kid should be taken on their own. It sounds fantastic on paper, but you end up with an uneasy student body. There is no pattern—always a question mark. [8]

A change in philosophy [has occurred]. The way things are done goes against the grain of smoothness that used to exist. [44]

Such a different philosophy. It is almost a reversal. [59]

When the new administration came in, they changed every administrator. We have a whole new game. [10]

The big change is the administration. It's hard to adjust to a difference in philosophy. [20]

We have given in too much. The administration has done that too much. [21]

The administration has the philosophy of ultimate democracy where everyone's [input] is treated exactly the same. It sounds fine on paper. [22]

Then the administration changed. The philosophy was different. It doesn't believe in applying rules equally to every kid. It sounds wonderful but the whole disciplinary framework is broken down. [23]

[The administrator] said he wanted the school to handle each kid differently, even if kids had done the same thing. It creates inconsistency. Kids know if they give a good story, they will get off. [35]

The administrative philosophy is oriented to the individual student. [37]

In saving one bad kid, we are sinking the good ones. [85]

The biggest cause of change is a difference in philosophy. [47]

The sheer repetition of the comments suggested that inroads were being made into the very core of the ethos that had evolved over the years. At one level, enforcement went against one of the three major tenets, and that would probably have been enough to elicit a strong negative response. But the emotion and almost near unanimity say that the faculty felt much more was at stake. Often the deep-rooted concern was inarticulable, a vaguely felt sense of uneasiness; however, others seemed to recognize clearly the greater threat to the foundations of the school's tradition.

I've talked to teachers who say they feel like kids are running the school. [40]

The real question is who is to run the school. I think [the administration] thinks kids should run it. You know the old saying, "If it ain't broke, don't fix it." [16]

The administration always sides with the kid. [76]

There is a prevailing attitude among students that they do have control. The staff feels it shouldn't have a power play with the kids. [45]

A lot of teachers feel like kids run the school. I'm not sure they're wrong. [48]

You don't ask kids if they want to be punished for being tardy. [12]

I believe in giving kids the opportunity to try something but not when I have the insight to know we're going in the wrong direction. They're allowed to drop-add courses; you can't set the rollbook until mid-October. I can understand, but it's out of control. [20]

Other teachers believed that the community and the potential of legal recourse drove many school decisions.

They aren't going to back you in front of parents. [42]

Good values and principles don't seem as regarded as what to do if you face a lawsuit. [56]

I think they're suit conscious; they don't get rid of kids who cannot handle classroom situations. A kid has a right to be taught. Those denying it should be removed. We have to get back to where the teacher controls the school. [21]

When the school gets one call from a parent, things are wild. [36]

The administration is very aware of the public image; when it comes down to that, the school goes with the parent's wishes. [38]

Sometimes in schools you have adversarial relationships, but the administrative position is what's going to keep the image clean, what's going to appease the community, satisfy the parent, or quiet down this very disobedient child. Sometimes, it's hard to work in that environment. [5]

Any time a decision is made, the first thing thought of is, will a lawyer be with parents? It's almost like parents run the school. [37]

Three staff members spoke for many concerning what they believed to be the proper locus of decision making.

For years this was a department-run school. That has changed. [19]

The experts on running the school are teachers. [41]

You want an immediate solution? Tell the administration and the state to leave the school and tell the school board and superintendent not to call the teachers. [3]

It was during discussions about discipline that almost all of the comments presented at the very beginning of this chapter were made. And discipline was always the first topic teachers brought up when asked the open-ended question, What changes have been made in the school? Its importance far outstripped what one would predict for a suburban school with a student body whose behavior, to outside observers and teachers new to the school, was generally unremarkable. As one relatively new teacher remarked, "I would say [to teachers who complain about student behavior]; believe me, this is a piece of cake" [45].

The discipline system caused teachers to question whether the classroom was still the capitol—that is, whether student learning was the ultimate touchtone for most decisions. They suspected that public relations and legal issues now guided judgment; the balance of control was shifting dramatically, from being centered around classrooms to being centered around community and student rights. In the process, teachers began to consciously realize that the second and third tenets discussed earlier were intricately entwined with the first. And the fabric woven over the years, in their minds, began to unravel.

THE SACRED AND CHANGE

Sarason (1971) convincingly argues that the culture of schools poses a considerable obstacle to change. Every alteration affects in some way an existing regularity in school functioning, be it norm, value, or practice. Reinforced by myth and ceremonies, those regularities become stubbornly entrenched. Often they are the force that repels the change, rather than the change being the force that alters operations.

It is important that not all of the changes that teachers faced were cultural, nor was the school's culture completely conservative. Acceptance of the Madeline Hunter program was readily given primarily because it meshed nicely with teachers' willingness to improve instruction. The program built on the sacred and was accepted by all and embraced by some as a result. The essential problem was to convince people that the program represented an important advance in the state of the art. Even the accountability-related changes were mostly accepted, albeit reluctantly. The apathetic responses, withdrawal, and refusal to cooperate were directed mostly at the changes that diverged the most from the tenet of the classroom as capitol. Resistance took on a different character as this normative aspect of life came under fire; it became not a matter of the mind but of the heart. In one circumstance, then, culture encouraged systematic progress; in another, it resisted change.

EPILOGUE

In the spring, teachers were asked how the situation at the school could be resolved. The answer was not clear to most; but reflecting a belief that the strength of the school was the faculty, the majority opinion argued that the faculty would ultimately be responsible for correcting the situation.

The following fall found a decidedly more upbeat faculty. Several adjustments in scheduling practices and in the discipline system conveyed a sense of increased order to teachers. In addition, last year's senior class, depicted as a particularly unruly cohort for years, was gone. A much more accommodative atmosphere prevailed, even in the face of a difficult contract dispute with the school board

Others remained more reserved. The cyclical nature of time in educational institutions is such that each new year begins with hopes renewed and enthusiasm regenerated. These teachers wanted to watch a while longer to determine if the sun was indeed beginning to rise again.

4

Somerville High School:
A School for Good Citizens

The deeply held values and beliefs of an organization are expressed in a perceptible overall ethos or culture. When viewed from afar or compared to other types of organizations such as hospitals, high schools all look very similar. When viewed up close, however, they have very different, distinguishing characteristics. Thus, culture varies across high schools.

This same logic applies to the school itself. Viewed holistically, a high school appears to express a fairly coherent, common set of values and beliefs. That apparent unanimity fades as the rich, detailed living and changing complexity of the organization become more and more vivid. This was a major theme in the Somerville case: uniformity and unanimity in cultural beliefs dissolved into the bustling, hectic, colorful and yet orderly life of the school.

A second theme was that the specific content of the school's culture represented a mixture of societal values and beliefs, the history and traditions of the school itself carried in the minds of "old-timers" and carefully taught to "new-comers," and the values and beliefs of the school's immediate neighbors. These three forces—society, the organization, and the local setting—interacted and intertwined, affected and were affected by one another, and resulted in a set of values and beliefs that characterized the school's culture.

One major aspect of the development of a fairly coherent

set of cultural beliefs at Somerville was the appointment of a new leader—a new principal—to the school about six years prior to this study. "The Boss" (as he was called by many) brought order to a school in crisis by drawing on, strengthening, and heightening already present faculty and neighborhood beliefs. During his tenure, he developed and sustained a school culture emphasizing order and discipline, and preparation for the world of work.

Indeed, Somerville's overall purpose was to create good citizens—decent, capable, hard-working graduates who were prepared for the world of work. This was accomplished through an emphasis on vocationally oriented courses, a strong control ethos, and a flattening of academic aspirations. Although some students went on to college and some dropped out of school altogether, these students were not as important as, for example, the business education students. Somerville, then, defined success as producing good citizens. Strongly expressed by teachers across departments, these beliefs had been drawn out by the leader, who had implemented procedures and plans that expressed them, selected people who shared these beliefs, and shaped school symbols, ceremonies, and rituals to reflect and reinforce this central tenet of the school's culture—to prepare good citizens for the world of work.

This belief derived in part from the larger society, in part from the neighborhood served by Somerville, and in part from the history and traditions of the school. Along with preparing teenagers for postsecondary education, one historic function of high schools has been to prepare students for work; thus, it is clearly quite legitimate as an overall purpose. Similarly, the neighborhood that Somerville served had strong work-oriented and control-dominated values. This neighborhood had a long history of close involvement in the life of the school, as did business and community groups. But more central was the role of the organization—the high school—and the teachers and administrators who expressed values and beliefs as they went about their daily work in shaping the school's culture, where order and preparation for the world of work were valued above all.

Order and preparation for work took on sacred qualities

at Somerville. They were the touchstones used to determine legitimate activity. But interestingly, they were not uniformly expressed throughout the faculty. The small group holding these values as sacred was referred to as the "Coterie." Extremely close socially and loyal to the principal, the Coterie enunciated the school's core values most clearly and most often. The majority of the staff adhered to expectations to emphasize discipline and order as the school's highest priorities but were willing to consider alternatives to a strictly vocational orientation. And there was a small group of "outsiders" whose commitment to the school and its values was marginal. Their orientation was often expressed as opposition to the principal and the values of order and work which he embodied. Thus, the normative elements of the culture, though widely shared, were sacred for the group wielding the most influence on school activity but were profane for a considerable portion of the faculty.

The school developed an inviolate sense of autonomy and independence from outside reform efforts. Recently, this attitude was challenged as new leadership in the city's school district administration began a series of initiatives intended to systematize teaching and monitor student progress closely. These efforts were viewed by Somerville's teachers as violating their fiercely guarded autonomy.

This chapter described the ethos of Somerville High School, the leader's role in drawing out this coherent set of beliefs, variation in that ethos among groups, and reactions to current outside challenges to this status quo.

THE SETTING

Metropolis, the large urban area where Somerville is located, is a city of neighborhoods. Sometimes ethnic, sometimes religious, always geographic, these neighborhoods are cohesive, tightly knit, stable, and often vocal about things that matter to them. One issue that matters is education. Many neighborhoods in Metropolis demand schools which reflect that neighborhood's values and beliefs—its culture. Local residents feel quite strongly that schools should reflect their beliefs about schooling. When the schools are no longer attuned to local culture, parents and other residents apply pressure to bring them back in line with local expectations. Sometimes pressure is directed towards the principal, sometimes toward teachers, and often towards "The Office," as the central administrative offices are called. Parents have so much clout that a teacher said, "It's easier for a parent to be heard [at The Office] than a teacher." In Metropolis, neighborhoods are listened to.

Somerville is a working-class neighborhood sitting high atop a ridge of land in the northwestern section of Metropolis. Economically and socially better off than the poorer neighborhoods that lie below it along the riverbank, Somerville was once prosperous by virtue of a large garment industry. Somerville residents now work in a variety of occupations. Modest, tidy row homes and twins (semidetached houses) line the residential sections of the neighborhood. Most homes are beautifully maintained and reflect the care and attention of their owners.

The business sections of Somerville are on Summit Avenue, the main street of the neighborhood. Small businesses and shops line several blocks of the avenue, and an occasional florist, restaurant, or tavern is located two or three blocks off Summit. Near the far end of Somerville's western boundaries (also the western boundaries of Metropolis) is an older shopping center which contains the discount branch of a large department store, a library, a movie theater, and a variety of clothing shops, pet stores, video shops, and drug stores. This shopping center marks the center of Upper Somerville, a subsection of the neighborhood. When describing where they live, parents underscore *Upper,* as if this word represents higher status than Somerville itself.

The high school sits on Summit Avenue between the main commercial area and the shopping center. The building and grounds occupy one full city block, and the football field is located in an adjacent block. The building is a three-story red brick building, built around 1925. The main entrance opens to a majestic, two-story marble entrance hall with mirror-image staircases on either side. Students are not allowed to use these marble stairs for entering or leaving the schools, or for passing between classes.

The entrance hall contains portraits of past principals of the school. When entering, one feels watched over by these individuals who have shaped the school. The landing on the second floor (the main floor) is decorated with large urns holding the school flag as well as the flag of Metropolis and the American flag. The current principal organized a ceremony when the former principals' portraits were hung. He invited the first president of the Home and School Association and the president of the first class to graduate from Somerville—the Class of 1907—to that ceremony. They sang the school song without having to read any lyrics—evidence of their loyalty to the high school.

At the time of the study, the school was populated by over sixty full-time regular teachers and over twenty special education teachers. In addition, there were nonteaching assistants, two full-time policemen, custodial staff, cafeteria staff, four guidance counselors, five secretaries, and four administrators. These adults were charged with a variety of responsibilities regarding the approximately 1,500 students who walked through the school's entrances every day. Of these, 250 were special education students bused in from various locations in and around the immediate neighborhood.

In the past decade, the school had undergone major changes: from a school where sixteen-year-olds reportedly skate-boarded down the hallways to one where boys removed their hats when they entered the building; from a high school with parents up in arms, "in revolt," as one teacher [24] described it, to one where parental and alumni contributions for sports uniforms, trips, and graduation prizes totals tens of thousands of dollars annually.

In the past, community discontent with the school ran high, teachers were apathetic, and the students had virtual license to do as they chose. Parents pressured The Office to provide them with new leadership, and eventually a new principal was assigned to the school. A significant part of the Somerville story details how that principal went about the complex work of rebuilding a coherent set of beliefs for the school. He was successful in this effort because he emphasized values reflecting those of the community and the teachers in the school. He viewed the school as a microcosm of society; "The school reflects the community. Some percent are flakes, some percent are thieves, some percent are solid—just like society." Ultimately responsible for the operation of the school, Mr. P was a masterful public speaker and a strong leader.

HISTORICAL BACKGROUND

Mr. Dunbar, the principal of Somerville before Mr. P, presided over some of the more turbulent times the school had endured. The early and mid-1970s were times of racial tension and violence, anti-government demonstrations, and the growing disenchantment of adolescents. Mr. Dunbar, as described by the teachers, was unable to meet these challenges actively. He was seen as a true gentleman, one best suited for life at a boy's prep school: "a gentleman of the old school" [27]. He was accused of never leaving his office to walk the halls of the school and of telling teachers whatever they wanted to hear at the moment and then later reversing what he had said. He "invited" students to obey rules and to keep the walls clean from graffiti. His philosophy of education stressed consensual decision making and the nonviolent resolution of problems. A courtly man whose leadership style belonged to places of decorum and consensus, Mr. Dunbar was at odds with the Somerville community. During his tenure, discipline eroded to the point that students played hockey in the hallways with empty milk cartons. Mothers could not understand why he appeared so two-faced, saying one thing at one time and something else at another. Fathers and local businessmen could not fathom his belief in talking things through and his retreats to the sanctuary of his office. They wanted a take-charge man who would set limits on the students, be active in the community, and be one of the boys at the local tavern.

Mr. Dunbar was promoted to a position in the central

office. Another principal was sent to Somerville but lasted only briefly: he was so disliked by the community that he had to leave. One teacher said, "The parents couldn't stand him so they dug up some dirt on him and he was out" [5]. A couple of months into the school year, Mr. P finally arrived. "This guy [P] won the Home and School [the parents' association] over in a week—no nonsense" [34].

A product of Metropolis schools, a local man from a similarly close-knit neighborhood, Mr. P sensed the atmosphere and knew what had to be taken care of first: discipline. For Mr. P the first order of business was order:

> [When I first came,] the parents were in revolt . . . My philosophy is that I think our teachers are the pros. They need the proper environment to teach in: it should be free of distractions and conducive to learning. My job, and the disciplinarians' job, is to remove someone disrupting class. Get the clown out. That doesn't help the clown, but it does help the others. They you have the counselors deal with the clown.
>
> We take care of discipline. We believe in the axiom that no child has the right to interfere with another child's right to an education. If they want to commit educational suicide, that's bad enough and we feel sorry. But educational homicide we won't tolerate.

Establishing order at Somerville High School was not achieved by focusing only on student behavior. Mr. P believed that "you've got to give the kids something to believe in, something to care about." Thus, in the process of rebuilding school spirit and establishing a discipline code and procedures to follow it up, Mr. P participated in shaping the school's culture—as expressed in symbols and behaviors—to be more in tune with community values, teachers' beliefs and preferences, and his own ideals about education.

THE INNER CIRCLE

A cautionary note is necessary here. High schools are not small organizations. With over one hundred teachers, administrators, and support staff, and nearly fifteen hundred students, Somerville is only an average-sized high school. If a school is to have a strong (coherent) culture, most people within the school have to express or agree with a set of core values. This was the case with the core beliefs at Somerville, although the degree of commitment to, attachment to, and belief in the leaders, the organization, and the cultural value of good citizenship varied among the staff members.

Three subcultural groups were identified during the research. Two were quite small and vocal, and the third consisted of the majority of the teachers. The groups varied in their adherence to the cultural values, beliefs, and assumptions expressed by Mr. P. Closest to him ideologically was a small, lightly knit core of teachers and staff members who strongly expressed the school's dominant values and revealed unwavering loyalty to Mr. P as the prime symbol and shaper of those values.

To this group, Mr. P was a high priest. It was quite powerful culturally, socially, and politically, and over the years its members had developed a strong dedication to Mr. P, to Somerville, and to one another. They gathered socially outside of school time, treated themselves to a special lunch on payday, and performed myriad chores and tasks associated with the everyday operation of a high school. Like an elite subgroup in any organization, these dedicated loyalists had a name for their group, shared daily rituals and common understandings, and through their intense cohesiveness and aura of specialness excluded others. This exclusion was not consciously deliberate but, just as with any clique of friends, it had that effect. This group, the "Coterie," was a powerful shaper and maintainer of the school's culture, and their loyalty to Mr. P was deep:

[When he came in,] he sensed no rapport between administration and faculty. He set a new ambiance, a new atmosphere. [24]

Mr. [P] is behind us—he will finagle to help us. There are principals who hang you, but not him. He stands behind us. [65]

I really think highly of Mr. P—he always looks for the best in people. I think you work harder for someone like that. [76]

He knows how to talk and handle people. He knows what to say to whom. He is an expert at that and that's a large part of administration. His presence is commanding. [34]

The second group consisted of the majority of the teachers interviewed. These people also believed in and expressed the dominant values of the school, their respect for Mr. P as an administrator was uniformly high, and they believed in their work. They did not, however, identify with Mr. P closely. They regarded the Coterie as a curiosity, an interesting anomaly, that did not affect their working lives profoundly:

The clique doesn't bother me. If I can go to him and channels are open, I feel ok. If he had to discuss everything with those people, then I would be upset. [46]

You're setting up an elite group. Those people are singled out for favors—for coffee, for special luncheons. He *is* reachable; it's not a question that he's not. When he first came, he won a lot of us over. A lot of us were leery but then this inner group formed. I guess they feel they need extra points. [50]

I pretty much do what I'm supposed to do. I guess there's a bit of favoritism but if you've been working with people a long time, you go with the ones you know. [57]

There was also a third group, quite small, who felt unsuited to life at Somerville. Either because of a lack of emphasis on academics, burnout, or personal feelings against Mr. P, these teachers felt angry or disinterested—they were ready to leave and suggested marginal commitment to the school. Mr. P once referred to these as "the lunatic fringe." Like the unstable neutrons in an atom ring, they were too far from the nucleus to be an integral part of it and were as yet unattached to another organization. One such teacher, relatively new to Somerville, could acknowledge that Mr. P was a strong disciplinarian but expressed anger over the Coterie: "[That inner circle] gets all the goodies and I don't believe that's fair. Schools need new blood . . . They are *his* people and no one else can break in. They are given the goodies because they've had them for years and because they expect it" [39]. A second described how he saw favors being allocated: "He doesn't want any problems with the union. Favors are handed out to the union or to his 'group.' [It's as if he says,] 'You wash my hands, I'll wash yours' " [51].

Thus, there were always degrees of commitment to and expressions of Somerville's dominant values. But viewed holistically, the organization showed an overall cultural emphasis on order and good citizenship.

DISCIPLINE AND ORDER

Throughout the school, discipline and order were palpable values. As students passed between classes, nonteaching assistants were on duty in the corridors to insure orderly movement. A total of five professional staff members provided the disciplinary function. And formal school activities such as graduation ceremonies stressed proper behavior and decorum with little room for deviation.

In describing the importance of discipline and order, teachers emphasized how crucial it was for them to know that students would be disciplined swiftly and, for the most part, consistently:

[The administrators] keep everything outside the classroom under control so things in the classroom are under control. That builds morale among the teachers. [71]

The students know they won't be trifled with. [54]

If it's something serious—fighting or a drug bust—the disciplinarian will rush it through to the principal. Why?

Well, number one, he considers discipline a top priority in the school; and number two, by inclination or experience, he gets involved directly. [13]

Now I had two pink slips already today . . . I had two girls in Advisory who didn't want to fill out a form so rather than me fighting with them, I sent them to [103] and they filled out the forms there. They [the disciplinarians] back you up on anything. [45]

This is a blue-collar neighborhood—it's tough. And the kids learn that at home, so you have to show them that you are tough. *Then* you can be delicate with them . . . You don't have to be big or a man. *That's* the magic. How the hell does one person, just with the lift of an eyebrow, show that this is the situation? [52]

Mr. P encouraged and reinforced these beliefs about what mattered most in the school. Having the right people in these critical disciplinary roles was crucial for the development of order as a central cultural value. Furthermore, policies and procedures were needed that reinforced the importance of discipline consistently. It was also essential that the right people be assigned responsibility for carrying out these policies and procedures. Mr. P acknowledged this fact: "There's one thing I will take credit for is putting the right person in the right job. I have some discretion in that, [although] it's negotiated with the Union."

At the time of the study, discipline was carried out by the dean of students and three teachers who staffed the discipline room and taught fewer classes as a result. In addition to these four was another teacher who handled daily tardiness. The dean of students was a soft-spoken man who had lived in the community for decades and knew many students' families well. When called upon to mediate a dispute, handle a fight, or calm down an upset child, the dean calmly entered the fracas, removed the student from the situation, and began to talk with him or her softly and sympathetically. He seemed to care about the students at Somerville, as the following observed incident indicates:

Shouts are heard outside the discipline room. Five or six students come in with one girl, holding her arms. The dean walks in, takes the girl over to a bench, asks her to sit down, while telling her friends to go back to their classes. He turns to the girl and asks softly: "What happened? Do you know this other girl [the one who started the fight]? Do you live near her? Have classes with her?"

The girl is pretty upset but can tell her side of the story. The dean asks her: "Do you want to go home? Do you want to see the nurse?"

The other girl is brought in by one of the disciplinarians. The dean talks to both, trying to find out what went on. He turns to me and says, "It was a 'he say I say' or a 'she say I say' type of dispute." He shrugs his shoulders . . . The girls are suspended but with some TLC. [Field notes]

As described above, the dean was assisted by three teachers who were part-time disciplinarians and taught a reduced roster. The nucleus was a pair of strong, burly, self-described conservatives ("I'm further right than Attila the Hun") who had worked together for several years and were best described as the "muscle" of the discipline team. Zealous in their work, these two were on the alert whenever they were on duty in Room 61 (the discipline room). On a moment's notice they jumped into action to take charge of a student disrupting class, cutting class, or more seriously, fighting or dealing drugs. Chronic class cutters were given a daily attendance report which had to be signed by each teacher each period and handed in at the beginning of the next day when a new one was issued. For chronic cutting, talking back to a teacher, or the more serious offense of fighting, the student was suspended. If accompanied by a parent, the student could be reinstated right away. And after five days, even without a parent, the student was automatically reinstated.

Despite their firm appearance, all the members of the discipline team often went out of their way to help "preferred" students out. The following event shows how much caring lay behind the firmness:

> Mr. Williams gets a phone call from a parent. Apparently it's about a student (the parent's kid) who used to be a good student but has slipped. Mr. Williams offered to meet with the parent, get out all the student's records, talk with the student's teachers to find out what's going on with the student. [Field notes]

Mr. P retained responsibility for many disciplinary actions, largely because it was important to him and because he had a reputation for doing it well. In addition to sending recalcitrant students to a special school for discipline problems or making forced transfer decisions, myriad actions expressed how discipline should be handled. In the following example, Mr. P stressed how discipline related to education. There had been a fire in one of the vocational education specialty areas the day before. Mr. P went down to talk to the class:

> Mr. P takes over the class to explain what they're going to do. He says, "We won't punish even though the kids were fooling around. We will educate because that's what schools are all about . . . I am part angry and part proud—angry as hell and proud of you all at the same time." [Field notes]

Apparently the students had reacted quite appropriately once the fire broke out. They had observed safety procedures, had used the right equipment to put out the fire, and had called for help. Mr. P let them know they had been both foolish and responsible. But, more significantly, he used the incident to teach the students rather than just discipline them.

Some teachers, however, expressed concerns about the emphasis on discipline and the strong-arm tactics. A few felt that the suspension system was abused and that it did not work to modify a child's behavior. Instead, it only removed the child from school. Some teachers felt that there should be alternative ways of handling both chronic and acute problems. One suggested an in-house detention system or special program:

I would like to see something done other than suspensions. It doesn't really help the student—it gives them a
vacation. I like in-house suspensions. At another school,
all the teachers gave the student work to do in the
in-house suspension room. I think the suspension system
is the worst in the world. It's crazy to have a system where
the student can bring himself back. [46]

Another concern came from one of the special education
teachers, who felt that special education students were treated
more harshly than regular students when sent to Room 103:
"Their policies for special ed and discipline are not good. They
concur with the disciplinarians and back them up. Once they
know a student is special ed, they ride him" [61]. Despite these
dissenting opinions, most teachers valued the discipline system
because it allowed them to get on with their work and created
an overall atmosphere of order.

In addition to valuing a strong, consistent, and ever-
vigilant discipline system, the teachers at Somerville stressed
orderliness and decorum in many aspects of daily life, notably
proper dress, respect for elders, and manners. Although a
formal dress code could not be enforced in the high school
(because of what staff members referred to as the "Student
Bills of Rights"), there were strong suggestions about what was
acceptable and unacceptable. As the weather turned warm in
the spring, a suggested dress code was written and delivered to
each homeroom. Some teachers taped it to their classroom
doors. The code included the following guidelines: students
should not wear shorts, crop tops, fishnet shirts, miniskirts,
and so on. When any of these appeared, the teacher or
administrator present raised an eyebrow or scolded the
student gently but firmly, sending the message that the
clothing was unacceptable.

Respect and proper manners were reinforced daily as
teachers requested that a student remove a hat or inquired
how someone was. This behavior was also reinforced at the
top. In the conference room one day, a teacher approached
Mr. P with a question or two. Mr. P seized that opportunity to
call the teacher's attention to a student's behavior and to make

clear how he (Mr. P) preferred the teacher to handle the situation. There had been an incident with a boy on the team which the teacher coached. Reports had reached Mr. P that the boy had cursed at the teacher [34]. He probed to discover if, in fact, the child had cursed:

Mr. P:	Did [the kid] curse at you?
Teacher:	I didn't hear him curse.
Mr. P:	Are you sure he didn't?
Teacher:	No, I didn't hear him.
Mr. P:	Because I heard that he did.
Teacher:	Nope. Like I said, I didn't *hear* him curse.
Mr. P:	Good. Then I won't pursue it. Because I was sure that if he *had* cursed in front of you, he wouldn't be playing on the team now.

Mr. P seemed to be signaling to the teacher that cursing was not acceptable, and he wanted to be sure the teacher would enforce that value. Thus, the idea of order broadly defined to include discipline and proper behavior, demeanor, and respect for others was conveyed in myriad ways throughout the everyday life of the school. From dress code to discipline procedures, from a strong discipline team to teachers who valued the support they received, the professional staff expressed a belief in strong discipline, good behavior, and orderliness.

The culture of order at Somerville was also found in highly organized procedures and well-rehearsed ceremonies. Despite the potential disruptions occasioned by the logistics of bringing together fifteen hundred adolescents and eighty adults on a regular basis, mornings at Somerville had a particularly well-organized quality to them. The main office had a long (twenty-five-foot) counter separating the secretaries' desks from the doors to the hallway, a bulletin board or two, and the teachers' mailboxes. To either side were a conference room (which opened into Mr. P's office) and one of the vice-principal's offices. Each morning, teacher and staff sign-in sheets were spread on the large counter. Next to the counter was a four-shelf bookcase on rollers containing the roll books for each advisory, or "Book," as the homerooms were called. As a teacher arrived, he or she signed in, took his or her advisory roll book (if he or she had one—not all did), and chatted with other teachers, the administrators, or the occasional student in the office area.

As teachers took their roll books and as 8:30 a.m. approached, the person overseeing this process began to list those teachers who might be late or absent and who had advisories that needed coverage, and to notify those teachers assigned floating coverage for that day where they could go. Because of this well-planned process, all the advisories were covered, students were not left unsupervised, and teacher absences and lateness were noted. This setup is typical of other procedures that showed how routines were well planned and well organized.

Graduation ceremonies provide an illustration of how the Somerville High School community thought through the importance of an event and what it stood for. At the June graduation ceremony, the list of students who had perfect or near-perfect attendance throughout high school and junior high school was read aloud by Mr. P. Clearly, attendance was highly valued. Students receiving scholarships for postsecondary education were considerably fewer than the perfect and near-perfect attenders. Moreover, in his congratulatory speech to the class, the principal observed that "even more important than the three Rs, the Class of 1985 has learned the three Cs— caring, commitment, and community."

The teachers responsible for preparing the seniors for graduation worked long, hard hours to insure a polished ceremony. One teacher not only conducted the choir but also rehearsed the graduates in how they would march, file into the bleachers, stand, remove their caps, sit during the ceremony, and leave the bleachers. These arrangements were elaborate and complicated because the graduates spelled out "1985" in their blue and white robes, and attention to exact seating was necessary for the proper effect. And that effect was stunning as the boys' dark blue robes formed the background for the girls' white ones, which spelled out the graduation year. Once seated, the graduates removed their caps in a series of four arm movements "conducted" by the choirmaster. At a signal, all right arms moved simultaneously.

The speeches and speakers were also carefully selected, rehearsed, and presented. At Somerville, two competitions were conducted by the English department—one for the two best written speeches, and another for three oral speakers. One speaker presented at Class Day; the other two gave the graduation speeches. The speakers were selected by a team consisting of the principal, the vice-principals, and the head of the English department. Students were coached by their English teachers, and all tried out on a single day using the same material. Conducted in the auditorium, each trial was scored by the committee members. When all were done, the committee retired to the principal's office, where, by averaging the scores and weighing other considerations (in a biracial school, having one white and one black student would be thoughtful), the selections were made. These students then rehearsed the speeches they would give, attending to timing, intonation, clarity, and expression. The result was that on graduation night, the speeches were smoothly delivered, contributing to an overall impression of attention to detail, polish, and seriousness of purpose that could only have been achieved through disciplined and well-organized procedures.

EDUCATION FOR TOMORROW:
WORK AND THE INDIVIDUAL

We turn out good kids. Many are able to get good jobs in business or industry. And we have a reputation for that. [14]

The importance of strong discipline and an emphasis on order were certainly ends in themselves at Somerville. However, they were also means: they helped make what went on in the classroom—learning—possible. If students cut class or were disruptive, no learning could occur. Proper discipline and orderliness, then, set the stage for the other core value of the school: to prepare students for the world of work. Education at Somerville focused on work-bound students. Although some students sought some form of postsecondary experience (college or university, vocational training school), the dominant educational value lay with vocationally oriented students.

The overall thrust of preparing students for work was apparent in the size and importance of the business education department. Largest of all the departments except special education, business ed offered courses that ranged from Typing 1 to Advanced Bookkeeping and covered Office Practice, Shorthand, Word-Processing, and so on. These courses developed marketable skills that students could use immediately after graduation in various jobs. The department also had two cooperative programs in which their best students worked part-time while finishing the requirements for graduation. One program had students attend classes for a week, then work for a week. In the other, students came to school early, finished their classes by noon or 1 p.m., and then worked in the afternoon.

Each year the business education department sponsored a Business Graduates' Day at which graduates of the department returned and told current students about their careers. Not all were recent graduates; for the 1985 Business Graduates' Day, several returnees had graduated five years previously. Local employers were more than happy to release a graduate for the morning. At least three teachers and two administrators mentioned how all the business education students had jobs by the time of graduation. This successful placement rate was due to the caliber of the students and to the history of successful placements with businesses and organizations in the metropolitan area.

There was some tension, however, both within the business education department and between that department and the traditional academic departments. Students enrolled in business education courses on an elective basis. However, newly mandated graduation requirements had reduced the number of electives available to high school students.

The new requirements stipulated an additional two years of science, one of math, and one of social studies. These additions to the already-required one year of science, two of math, two of social studies, four of English, and four of physical education and health significantly reduced the number of electives students could take. One teacher indicated, "With the various requirements, we have sixteen out of twenty-one. That leaves only five electives and students need about eight—two or three a year—to get adequate skills" [10].

In the spring, members of the business education department were struggling with the implication of this situation for their survival, viability, curriculum, and relationship with other departments. At a special committee meeting, three business teachers discussed how the new requirements reduced the students' flexibility in selecting courses and favored the college-bound students. Since so few of Somerville's students attended college, teachers' concerns focused on the majority of the students—those who needed business electives to learn skills that would help them get jobs. The recently appointed department head described the requirements as "short-sighted." He said, "Not every student needs academic preparation. Other skills are necessary for students who are [then] fully prepared to go on to work" [10].

Concern was also expressed about the substitution of, for example, business math for regular math and business English for regular English. Teachers believed that, under the new requirements, this practice could continue, although students would be able to substitute only one English and one math course.

The business education department received the administration's full support and approval. As the department head felt,

[One unusual thing at Somerville] is the acceptance and enthusiasm of other people for the Business department. In some schools, the principal feels he should have an "academic school," regardless of the skills of the students.

Thus, the business ed department was the flagship department in the school and the most collegial in terms of faculty members' relations with one another. The teachers described how they worked together and learned from one another:

> I believe we have such excellent teachers because we all work together so well. [3]

> Everything I've learned about organization I've learned here. [The department head] and the other teachers helped me out enormously here. They all came to help me out. [39]

> We're like a family. We have communication; and we have strong leadership. In this department, we go beyond the ordinary, like we try to place all the seniors [in jobs]. This increases our morale enormously . . . We will sacrifice a lunch period, we stay after school—we don't mind doing that. We also work together during department meetings. [46]

> One thing you learn is that you can only do so much. We do the best with what we're given but what makes this department good is that we don't cheapen the department—we have our standards. [38]

This cultural value of preparing students for the world of work was also expressed in a strong concern for the individual rather than for some academically driven standards or performance criteria. Teachers paid attention to the student and his or her uniqueness, rather than to the precepts of a particular academic subject area.

In describing their work, the teachers emphasized the individual child and meeting his or her needs so that each one would derive something useful for general citizenship and for tomorrow's world. One teacher [24] developed this idea as follows:

> Q: Now let's talk about you. What are your goals when you teach?

A: I'm not teaching [subject]; I'm teaching the kids. It's a multigoaled theory because each kid doesn't have the same aspirations, goals, or ability. It depends on each child. There are several hundred kids I keep in touch with. You can't see them as clones; each one will take what you say differently.

And another described this value as follows:

You have to know them personally. You have to know who forgot his or her glasses; you overhear them talking about square dancing; you have to understand that the boys were thinking about a soccer game today . . . I adjust my teaching, depending on the level of the class. [25]

Accommodating the individual was also expressed by a business education teacher [3] who described two situations in which individual adjustments had to be made to meet an employer's needs. In one, a co-op student was needed for a whole month straight (rather than one week at work, one week at school) because a secretary was sick. The teacher described that they were able to adjust the student's roster so that there would not be any problems. In a second incident, the employer needed the student to begin a job at the end of May rather than a couple of weeks later after graduation. Once again, the teacher believed that they would be able to accommodate to the needs of the employer and the desires of the student.

Roster changes at Somerville also reflected a deep commitment to meeting the needs of the individual student. Although not a large high school, Somerville ranked high across the city in the absolute number of roster changes made each year. Teachers felt that this practice was valuable and the way things should be. Said one, "That's one of the values of [Somerville]. We have a lot of roster changes but that means we can accommodate to the child" [25]. Moreover, roster changes were made late in the school year if they made sense for the student. One day in February, one of the four guidance counselors approached an administrator with a problem. The student involved had requested a roster change in December, but the request had not been acted on. Apparently it had been misplaced somewhere along the approval route. The administrator suggested that the counselor get the department head's approval; if he approved it, the administrator would go along, too. The department head happened to enter the main office just then. When he heard what had happened, he said "No problem," signed the change form, and commented on what a shame it was for the student to have to wait so long.

Other sorts of problems were often resolved to the benefit of the student. One April incident involved an apparent senior, "apparent" because the problem arose as to whether or not she had the proper credits to graduate. She had bounced around from school to school—a private school, a magnet high school—and finally had landed at Somerville in the Alternative Program, a structure designed for students who needed more support and routine in their daily lives than the typical high school student. Described as an art major and a "neat kid," the girl had been in a senior advisory all year and had been led to believe she would graduate. She had paid her class dues, which covered prom, graduation, and yearbook expenses. Mr. P had established the policy that senior students who were in a senior advisory and had passed all the necessary courses would graduate. The girl was in an Alternative Program advisory, had passed all her courses, and was on all the graduation lists. However, because she had attended several schools, it was not clear that she had the proper credits. Mr. P exclaimed that he could not tell her, in April, that she was not going to graduate, but he was very angry at the person who had let the situation develop. The roster chairman was called in to verify the credit transfer procedures. A thoroughly well-organized and precise man, he demonstrated how he had transferred the credits from the girl's other schools and that they were adequate for graduation. Had her credits been just under the required number, Mr. P would have resolved the problem in the student's favor.

Mr. P also moved among the students and the faculty to break down the anonymity that can exist in high schools. Each day he walked all the hallways of the school, greeting teachers, picking up the odd piece of trash, noting where the plaster was peeling. Teachers and students saw him, knew he was there, and he saw them. (A recent illness has cut down the frequency of these walks.)

> Mr. P is around all the time. He walks the halls and puts his head in. The kids wave at him. [45]

> He walks the halls, he's around the school, he pokes his head in the classroom. [46]

> He makes his presence felt—he's all over the building . . . He checks on the kids in the halls, asks them where they're going, if they have a pass. [14]

Mr. P especially tried to make the students feel known and cared for. For example, the hockey team had been raising money for two years to attend a major tournament in England. The day before they left, although he had been quite ill, Mr. P came to school especially to wish them well and to urge them to conduct themselves in ways that would reflect well on the school, the city, and the country; he urged them to show that they were exemplary Somerville, Metropolis, and American citizens.

CHALLENGES TO AUTONOMY

As part of a large urban school system, Somerville High School had to develop a unique personality, a set of characteristics that set it apart from the other comprehensive city high schools. One such characteristic was a fiercely guarded and zealously defended sense of autonomy. This belief had been tacitly promoted by a recent central office administration that was uninvolved in school operations and that had encouraged such an attitude.

Two years before the study began, this placid status quo was challenged by the appointment of a forceful, assertive new superintendent. Dr. Salomon began a series of school improvement reforms intended to raise standards, to prod teachers and students to be more accountable, and to bring order and coherence to a fragmented curriculum. His initiative had two main features of concern to Somerville's teachers: a standardized curriculum and a pacing schedule.

Because of Somerville's predominant work ethic, any reform stressing academics was bound to create consternation. As with the new graduation requirements discussed above, teachers at Somerville responded to Dr. Salomon's initiatives with dismay. They saw the standardized curriculum as robbing them of their authority to make classroom decisions and as usurping their responsibility to design an educational program for their students.

A majority of teachers rejected the very notion of a standardized curriculum for an entire city and used every opportunity they found to ridicule the locally developed tests. This dismay and ridicule apparently arose from their emphasis on valuing the individual student. They very concept of designing classroom experiences that were basically similar for all students was anathema. This belief was reflected in community members' strong support of the high school as a unique place, unlike any other in the city. Parents thought that the notion of the pacing schedule was absurd. During a parent-sponsored brunch honoring teachers, one parent remarked, "I think that the idea that everyone should be doing exactly the same thing all across the city on any one day is stupid . . . Each school is different and each teacher is different . . . Don't they know that down there [in the district central administrative offices]?"

Several teachers expressed anger at having to follow a curriculum written by central office staff that was intended for all students in Biology 1 across the city, for example. They felt that this policy in no way responded to the needs of Somerville students as a group and violated their strongly held belief about the school's and their professional autonomy. As one teacher lamented, "I think it's wrong to mandate the maximum—what you have to pass—instead of the minimum . . . Each school needs to be individualized" [45]. Another described how Somerville had initiated curriculum revisions that preceded the central office's revisions. With some pride, she noted the following:

> The business ed department had incorporated the standardized curriculum before it became mandatory. We made some changes because we felt things were obsolete and we needed to update them . . . We do have individual differences and my greatest concern is for those who won't meet the competencies. [46]

One latent concern about the district change initiatives was their strong academic bias. Clearly there were certain risks for teachers to express antiacademic opinions, but muffled grumblings and whispered conversations about the set of reforms indicated that teachers felt these initiatives were all wrong for the students they taught. As in the Monroe case, a "psychological development" perspective appeared to be valued in Somerville as well: the teachers construed their overwhelming responsibility as determining where the student was and teaching from that level on, and not as insisting on some set of lessons prescribed for this particular day for this particular course, regardless of the students' readiness.

Moreover, Somerville's valuing of order and the world of work above all else contained an anti-intellectual tone. Teachers hinted at this attitude by saying, "One of the best-kept secrets here is homework . . . Have you [the researcher] heard anyone talk about homework since you've been here?" Another teacher corroborated this observation by pointing out the reluctance of several teachers to take on the Senior Advanced Placement classes because of the time and intellectual demands needed to prepare for such a class.

The teachers' fiercely guarded sense of professional autonomy came through in a discussion with a very bright, articulate math teacher. In describing her and other teachers' reactions to the standardized curriculum, she recalled the 1950s and 1960s before the district was unionized:

> Some of what's going on now under Dr. Salomon reminds us of that time when administrators could force things on

teachers. It's not so much the content; it's the way it's being done. So many things are being forced on us without our input. We don't like it. [62]

Another teacher in the same department echoed these perceptions:

There is no formula for anything. No formula works in any area . . . The standardized business isn't being resisted; it's a matter of the way it's being handled. Apparently the powers-that-be have little respect for teachers because they have said you can't handle this so we will. [52]

As a group, the Somerville teachers scorned the centrally initiated reform effort because it did not respect the needs of Somerville students and did not respect the teachers' professional status. Although many felt that the specific content of the new curricula was acceptable, a heavy-handed, top-down reform process made them angry and defensive.

Although early reactions to what was perceived as a heavy-handed, top-down reform initiative were strong, it was too early to ascertain if teachers' responses would be as strong as those in Westtown or if teachers and the community would unite into a culture of opposition at Monroe. As a group, Somerville teachers scorned the reform initiatives. For some, especially the Coterie, they did so because the reform challenged their attitude toward the individual students and the sacredlike expectation that their purpose was to prepare students for the world of work. For other teachers, less tenacious in their adherence to order and work norms, the specific content of the reforms might have been acceptable if the implementation process had been more respectful of teachers' knowledge and experience; a heavy-handed, authoritarian process left them feeling angry and defensive. Resistance to district reform, then, appeared to be beginning to take on a uniformly strong character. The reasons behind this resistance, however, varied. The Coterie would probably defend the school and its sacred values of order and the world of work against any challenge from the outside; other staff members would be willing to consider the changes if a more democratic procedure were used.

In his role as cultural leader, Mr. P served as a buffer from this authoritarian initiative and as an interpreter of it. In words and gestures, he conveyed to teachers that they were "the pros," that he regarded them highly as professionals, and that the central office was very removed from the realities of everyday life in schools. In the words of one teacher: "He lets us know that some is rhetoric—there's only so much you can do. He makes us feel that we know the kids best and that what we do on a daily basis is best for them" [62].

Toward the beginning of the next school year, an additional curricular reform began to spread through the city schools. This writing initiative was funded through outside monies and was to be implemented in a few schools each year. At a general faculty meeting, Mr. P introduced the idea and then made the following remarks: "What do we need people coming in from the outside telling us what to do? We don't need that. We *know* [emphasis added] what we're doing here at Somerville" [19]. And so did just about everyone else.

Of the three high schools studied, Somerville had the most uniformly shared set of cultural norms when the community, building administration, and faculty were considered. Through substantive decisions and symbolic expression, most people in the school valued order and preparation for the world of work as their predominant education goals. However, these values appeared to be sacred only for the Coterie, and the researchers' expectation was that any challenges to the norms would be deflected or encapsulated by this group. This was becoming evident at the study's end, as teachers and administrators began to openly formulate their opinions on the district's improvement initiatives. However, to be sure, the entire reform process would have to be followed. It seems likely that, in the long run, the "School of Good Citizens" would not give up easily the central, often tacit, tenets of its culture.

5

Culture and Change

The classroom as an instructional sanctuary. The integrity of professional specialities. Order and citizenship. West-town, Monroe, and Somerville faculty members each held resolutely to different core values. Each reacted differently to challenges to these values. And each measured progress using different benchmarks of effectiveness. The preceding stories underscore in bold lines the occasionally subtle but nevertheless critical cultural variety that existed among the schools.

But the variety yields some coherence. The three stories point toward several general statements about school culture. Although obviously not universal generalizations, these statements mark the beginnings of a grounded theory that accounts for school-to-school variance in cultural makeup and faculty reactions to planned changes. This chapter presents three statements on each topic and then concludes on a speculative note with observations about the relationship between behavioral and cultural change in schools.

VARIATIONS IN LOCAL SCHOOL CULTURES

The first three of the statements characterizes the composition and texture of school culture by addressing the sources of

121

shared expectations in a school, the extent to which the norms are known and adhered to, and the tenacity with which they are held.

Statement 1

A school culture, the set of shared expectations about what is and what ought to be, derives from both the more distant external environment common to most schools and the local setting.

Numerous educational observers have commented on the conditions of schooling and the teaching occupation that have made educational practice remarkably similar from generation to generation and from community to community. According to these accounts, neither time nor place greatly affects teacher sentiments about their occupation (Lortie, 1975), instructional supervisory practices (Meyer & Rowan, 1977), boredom and time spent waiting (Jackson, 1968), student achievement (Coleman, 1966), or organizational structure (Miles, 1981). Yet other authors have spelled out the variations within and among schools, including organizational structure across schools (Schlechty, 1976), organizational structure between levels (Herriott & Firestone, 1984), departmental structure within schools (Wilson & Corbett, 1983), student achievement (Rutter et al., 1979; Brookover, 1979), and the relationship between school program and culture (Metz, 1986). The lines of inquiry are not contradictory. Rather, the issue is one of figure and ground. From a distance, sameness overwhelms; from closer up, variation is striking.

It is important to distinguish between two types of norms that coexist in schools: universal and local norms. Universal norms, borrowing from Williams's (1970) discussion, are those that are shared by most group members—in this instance an occupational group. They derive from the commonalities that surround anticipatory socialization, actual induction, and eventual occupational practice. Thus, common denominators buttress definitions of what the occupation is and ought to be.

However, the practitioner works in a particular community, in a particular building, and in a specialized department where the constant interaction of rules, roles, and relationships generates more idiosyncratic views of what is true and good. The mixture of universal and local norms that come to be known about and adhered to, then, helps define the culture in individual settings.

The contribution of occupationwide and setting-specific definitions was demonstrated in Westtown, Monroe, and Somerville. Local norms dominated instructional practice at Westtown and Somerville, although, in talking to teachers there, researchers also heard comments that reiterated nationwide themes. For instance, teachers' concern that principals should support them in disciplinary matters appeared in both schools and echoed a frequently noted theme in discussions of teachers' views of their work (Lortie, 1975; McPherson, 1979). Definitions of teaching at Monroe were the product of individuals' occupational induction, especially their immersion into a specialty. Teachers' frustrations arose when their perceptions about student's achievement and attitudes toward school did not fit the teachers' assumptions. Monroe's dramatic transformation from a school where students had a wide range of demonstrated achievement to one with a more skewed distribution punctuated the discrepancy between national expectations and local conditions. The influence of the local setting at Somerville was quite dramatic in terms of definitions of the purpose of schooling and the proper relationships among staff and students; instruction had been less affected. The point is that the culture of each school was composed of universal themes interpreted in light of local events and conditions; this mix defined the important expectations for each school and gave it its unique character.

Statement 2

Schools vary in the uniformity of their school culture, that is, which norms are widely known and followed.

The discussion of statement 1 illustrates how the content

of the norms varies form school to school. Equally important, the extent to which these norms are held in common can also vary. School cultures, then, are different in their uniformity.

Westtown had a highly uniform teacher culture. Not only were most norms shared by most teachers, but the school had no clearly identifiable subgroups that valued behavior contrary to the widely held norms. The case study noted some divergent views, but none challenged the core tenets, and they were individually held. Indeed, those with divergent perspectives usually described themselves as isolated or were observed to be such. Somerville's was the most uniform *school* culture; yet its central tenets were distributed differently from those in Westtown. Expression and reinforcement of norms about preparing students to be productive citizens were most evident in the principal's behavior and were mirrored by teacher subgroups to varying extents, to the greatest extent by the Coterie and to the least extent by those at the fringes. Faculty acceptance of the norms and devotion to the charismatic leader were patterned in a series of concentric circles. Monroe's culture was the most diverse. The case description portrays a faculty that agreed to disagree on its views of appropriate teaching and what should be taught. These differences led to variation in acceptance of new practices. More uniformity in expectations for appropriate teacher-administrator relation-ships was apparent.

The above discussion indicates the importance of school subcultures. As chapter 1 notes, an organizational culture is not monolithic. A group or groups within a school may hold definitions of what is and what ought to be that are different from those held by other groups in the school. The presence of subcultures may reflect a number of conditions: a single deviant subculture that resists a strong central culture; one or more divergent subcultures that emerge because the central culture fails to carry a quality of obligation that compels others' actions; or the presence of several groups that hold different beliefs about some central issue. These possible patterns illustrate the importance of avoiding the "holistic fallacy" or expectation that a school culture is uniformly held.

Statement 3

Norms vary in the extent to which staff members perceive them as alterable.

This statement points to the sacred and profane characteristics of norms. Some norms are untouchable and exempt from tampering, and others are more pliant. This resilience is the consequence of sacred norms being positioned at the core of teacher's professional identities and being more than a preferred way of believing and behaving—they are *the* way. The sacredness of norms is independent of the uniformity with which they are held: that is, profane norms can be widely accepted as definitions of what is true and good and yet group members also can be open to changing these expectations for behavior; group members cannot even conceive of functioning under alternatives to sacred norms. Nevertheless, it may be that only a small group in the total population holds a norm as sacred.

To illustrate, from all available evidence, the tenet of the classroom as the capitol at Westtown was uniformly held and sacred; it was accepted by almost all faculty members and provided their raison d'être. At Somerville, the exception that the purpose of the high school was to produce good citizens was sacred to the principal and his Coterie—that is, it was the purpose of the school and thus intimately tied to who they were as educators; but other staff members, although accepting it, did not view it as the only possible definition of schooling. And, for a few, it was clearly not the best possible alternative. Thus, the norm was widely shared and yet its sacred quality was upheld mostly by what might be called the "high priest" and the close circle of believers. The norms that were most sacred and compelling to teachers at Monroe were often held by a subgroup. For instance, teachers holding the academic perspective persisted in teaching a college preparatory curriculum for over a decade in spite of evidence that students were failing that curriculum and did not benefit from it and in the face of pressure from administrators to adjust to a changing clientele. These teachers' identities were inseparable from their content specialty.

An additional note is that the essential qualities of cultural norms in a school, their uniformity and their sacredness, may not be attributes that staff members can verbalize easily. Westtown and Monroe staff members did not consciously recognize how valuable certain expectations were until a challenge to them arose (for example, the new administrative philosophy toward discipline at Westtown and the basic skills instructional push at Monroe). The threats established what the normative boundaries were—the limits to what was acceptable as true and good. Thus, to say that norms are widely shared or not subject to tampering is not to say that staff members are conscious of these boundaries.

FACULTY RESPONSES TO CHANGE

The second set of statements depicts how culture tempers a staff's reactions to change and its acceptance of new expectations.

Statement 4

The aversion to change varies with the character of the norms challenged and the newness of the challenge.

Aversion means more than *resistance,* a term that implies behavioral opposition. Adopting an adversarial posture may be an overtly dramatic response to change, but aversion means more than that. It means distaste and repugnance; it conjures up an image of an emotional, deeply felt reaction. Therefore, aversion also includes the mental and physical health implications of an attempt at change. Indeed, a frequent indicator of a perceived attack on the sacred were comments that people felt they had to leave the school or that they could no longer function according to their own ideas of what teaching should be.

This type of response is reserved for innovations that

tamper with sacred norms. Culture is most conservative when efforts toward change bump into those expectations. Data from the Westtown case best support this statement, but the case is interesting because it shows the same group's reactions to three changes that differed in the extent to which they challenged an apparently sacred norm. The emotional and physical accompaniments to opposition were clearly tied to threats to the classroom as capitol. Staff members could distinguish among their responses to changes related to Madeline Hunter techniques, accountability, and discipline; reactions were most averse with the last.

At Monroe norms that were sacred to subcultures had been under attack for over a decade because of changes in the student body, special programs, and administrative personnel. The level of aversion was somewhat, but only somewhat, lower than at Westtown because teachers had developed ways to cope. Some of these were individual adaptations that allowed compliance with the most observable portions of innovations—like the schedules in the QTPs—and still made it possible to cover the content that teachers found fundamentally important to their perspectives of good teaching. Other coping strategies included cultural modifications, like the belief that administrators and their programs come and go but teachers remain; the teachers' professional boundaries excluded administrators.

The comparison of Westtown and Monroe suggests a natural history of how attacks to sacred norms are handled in schools. Aversion is strongest early in the process while the attacks are fresh. If these attacks are not reversed, some people will leave. Others will develop ways to stay in the situation and continue to do what they consider as fundamental to their raison d'être. These coping behaviors will include strategic compliance and the erection of defenses against the attackers. The result will be a subculture of opposition that offers some comfort for those who remain. The price of such a development may well be a more reserved teacher commitment to the school; indeed, Westtown staff members already acknowledged that the level of enthusiasm for working at the school that existed a few years ago would be difficult to regain.

Statement 5

Behavioral change is possible through frequent communication of new definitions of what is and ought to be and
close enforcement of these expectations.

Monroe teachers, many of them at least, changed their
behavior despite expressed opposition. The reasons for this
change can be traced to the supervisory changes accompanying
the mandated change, increased monitoring, and the repetitive
emphasis on the required behavioral changes over the last few
years. Staff members knew what was expected, and they
regularly came into contact with administrators in such a way
that change-related behavior was visible. The Somerville
principal achieved the same results, although the particular
strategies he used were more difficult to retrieve. Nevertheless,
reconstructions of the formative period suggest that the
principal's view of what schooling should be were constantly
reiterated in action and comments to staff members. Continual
reinforcement of this view was still in place and was given more
through informal encouragement than formal supervision and
more through ceremony than evaluative conferences. On the
basis of those two experiences, one would expect successful
implementation of Madeline Hunter techniques at Westtown.
The "buzz words" were constantly mentioned, and formal
evaluation was beginning to take note of whether the related
practices were showing up in the classroom.

These cases fit well with the literature on occupational
socialization, that is, the process through which a neophyte
becomes acquainted with the definitions of what is and ought
to be in a group. Numerous research studies describe the
highly interactive process through which behavior is shaped
(Brim and Wheeler, 1966; Simpson, 1979; Bucher and
Stelling, 1977). The discussion of Williams (1970) in chapter 1
also highlights the fact that a culture's normative system is
defined not only by the knowledge of and adherence to norms
but also by the processes of transmitting and enforcing them.

Statement 6

Behavioral change may be a preliminary to cultural change, but it does not insure acceptance of desired new norms.

Cultural change is the acceptance or internalization of new definitions of what is and what ought to be. A considerable body of research suggests that attitudes follow from behavior (Breer and Locke, 1965; Fullan, 1985); in the same way, behavioral change is probably a preliminary to cultural change. However, behaviors are like symbols in one crucial respect: the meaning is not inherent in the act or artifact itself (Eliade, 1959). Instead, meaning is socially constructed through collective interpretive processes.

Where the change in question is planned—or at least part of a conscious reformative effort—the extent to which cultural change occurs and is in the intended direction will depend on both the interpretive activities of the leaders of the change and available elements in the culture to be modified. Here the most telling comparison is between Somerville and Monroe. At Somerville, Mr. P embarked upon a transformative effort designed to modify the school's culture. This modification was in fact an intensification of themes that already had a sacred quality to both faculty and the community. Through his own statements and manipulations of symbols such as during the graduation ceremony, he clarified existing values of the importance of order, citizenship, decency, and preparation for the world of work. The new culture reflected and institution-alized this intended direction of change.

The superintendent in Monroe district initiated an additive change process by which attitudinal changes would be welcomed but were secondary to behavioral change. The intent of this change—improvement of student test scores and basic skills achievement—was contrary to sacred values of many teachers. They argued that such improvement was not part of their job. The means used violated teachers' understandings of the complexities of classroom life and appropriate administrative-teacher behavior. Moreover, the school's culture already provided interpretations for this sort of behavior—"administrators come and go," "they do not understand us"—that allowed teachers to adopt specific behaviors without internalizing the values intended to go with them. Thus, behavioral change did not lead automatically to cultural change; compliance was not tantamount to acceptance.

OBSERVATIONS ON BEHAVIORAL AND CULTURAL CHANGE

Statement 6 has a negative tone to it, primarily because it sticks closely to the cases. Speculative straying from the data allows a recasting of the relationship between behavioral and cultural change in a more positive frame. Cultural change is most likely under certain circumstances. First, the behavioral change must challenge existing norms and values. The Madeline Hunter program at Westtown required behavioral changes, but since it was congruent with the local belief that the classroom is the capitol, no new definitions of teaching were needed. All other examples of changes in this study, however, implicated the existing culture, either by challenging it, as in the case of Westtown's discipline policy, or by building coherence in it, as happened at Somerville.

Second, the stage for cultural change may be set by a dramatic event, such as a drastic student population shift (Monroe), acute outbreaks of unruly student behavior (Somerville), severely disappointing test scores (Monroe and Westtown), or the arrival and departure of administrators (all three). During such critical periods in a school's life, alternatives to already-held definitions of what is and ought to be present themselves visibly and often necessitate a conscious questioning of the current norms, beliefs, and values. Essentially, crisis creates opportunity (assuming the current situation warrants changing and there is a state worth changing to). Whether the opportunity is seized depends at least partially on whether the promise of the restoration of order resides in new definitions rather than in old ones and whether leadership uses the symbolic, ceremonial, and ritualistic tools at its disposal to facilitate the attachment of meaning to the new norms. Somerville is the best positive example of this process. There, what was held sacred by a few was nurtured and built upon until a dominant coalition was formed. At the other two sites, existing norms were reaffirmed in the face of threats. In both, teachers thought the test score crisis was less important than administrators did. Not coincidentally, administrators at these sites relied almost solely on technical and political devices to promote proposed changes and eschewed the more culturally oriented means invoked by Mr. P.

Third, a considerable period of time must be available for the subsequent interpretive process—the give and take among conscience, intentions, and actions—to take place. The changes at Somerville had been institutionalized after six years of nurturance, encouragement, a dollop of hand slapping, and a heavy dose of symbolic activity. Practices that challenged existing norms at Monroe and Westtown remained unaccepted after more than two years. Clearly, the sacredness of the norms under challenge was also of critical importance. This research contained no instances, or even hints, of the sacred being changed. And in all probability this situation would continue until changes in the composition of the staff altered the balance among people that shared particular sacred norms. Active recruitment, self-selection in and out of the organization, and forced retirement probably will prove to be the most viable means for watering down the kind of subculture of opposition that developed at Monroe or the aggregate tenacity with which Westtown staff held some norms. In other words, sacred norms are less likely to change than is the composition of those who share the norms.

The complexity of the relationship between behavioral and cultural change highlights and elaborates the context-specific nature of planned change in education (Berman, 1981; Corbett, Dawson, and Firestone, 1984): that is, the same change is likely to be implemented in different ways and modified in different directions from setting to setting because of important but sometimes subtle differences in the local culture. In effect, the meaning of the change must be reconstructed at each location, and that reconstruction will be shaped substantially by local understandings about the appropriate means and ends of education.

The well-noted lack of continuation of many educational changes is most likely a telling comment on this tenuous connection between behavioral and cultural change. The disappearance of an innovation after the removal of special support for it says that the internalization of expectations for behavior has not occurred or, as was the case at Monroe, the norms internalized were not ones that would maintain the behavioral changes. The literature on continuation points directly to the importance of incentives, time for learning, and the institutionalization of rules, procedures, and evaluation as mechanisms to promote lasting change (Corbett, Dawson, and Firestone, 1984; Huberman and Miles, 1984). Listing these elements is another way of specifying the kind of interaction that supports new behavior and contributes to the development of a congruent culture. Where changes are not institutionalized, they do not "fit" the existing expectations. In such instances, the differences between behavior and cultural change becomes the difference between a momentary aberration and lasting reform.

6

Culture and Effectiveness

Recent research in education and business suggests that a unified culture specifying a clear mission contributes directly to organizational effectiveness (Deal and Kennedy, 1982; Rutter et al., 1979). This assertion is part of a larger debate in education and elsewhere about what *causes* organizational effectiveness and whether factors that can be said to create or contribute to that condition have been adequately identified (Purkey and Smith, 1983; Rowan, Bossert, and Dwyer, 1983).

At the same time that educators continue to concern themselves with how to make schools more effective, in other areas of organizational study attention has turned to defining the term *effectiveness* (see Goodman, Pennings, et. al., 1977). Although ambiguity still reigns, it has become clear that effectiveness cannot be defined empirically or logically. The definition adopted depends upon the definer's values and beliefs about what is important for the enterprise at hand (Scott, 1977). A wide range of criteria has been advocated. In education these criteria include student achievement, student and staff happiness or satisfaction, attendance, and job placement. In business the list includes productivity, efficiency, profit, market share, quality, growth, morale, control, adaptation, and stability. Researchers' empirical efforts to reconcile or rank these diverse criteria have been singularly unsuccessful (Mohr, 1982).

From a cultural perspective, these efforts are significant because they highlight how definitions of effectiveness flow from norms, beliefs, and values concerning the way things ought to be. This connection suggests a different and even more fundamental relationship between culture and effectiveness than previously considered in the literature: culture *defines* effectiveness. Extreme variation in definitions of effectiveness, then, most likely reflect variation in organizational cultures about what is important and worth striving for, about what is true and good, and about what is sacred.

One way to illustrate this argument is to examine the definitions of effectiveness embedded in the cultures of the three schools described here. Such an examination shows considerable diversity. The fact that diversity exists, however, does not mean that all definitions should be equally acceptable. The acceptability of one particular definition over another is a culture-bound, value-laden assessment. To offset the suggestion of cultural relativism, the next section offers some perspectives on what an acceptable range of local definitions of effectiveness might be.

DEFINITIONS OF EFFECTIVENESS

The socially accepted purposes of American secondary education are quite broad. Conant's codification (1959) of the comprehensive ideal suggests three objectives for high schools: to provide a general education for all future citizens, to provide programs that prepare students for work directly after high school, and to provide college preparatory programs for those who wish to continue their education after high school. More recently Goodlad (1984) argues that high schools, like other schools, should balance concerns for intellectual, personal, social, and vocational development. If anything, the range of objectives for high schools has expanded since the 1950s through a growing concern for the physically, mentally, socially, and economically disadvantaged. In fact, there is currently considerable confusion about what high schools should accomplish. In an effort to be all things to all people, the "shopping mall" high school has been created. This organization provides a wide range of options but provides little guidance as to the appropriateness of each option for a given student, thus throwing the problem of choice back on the individual learner (Powell, Farrar, and Cohen, 1985).

This multitude of goals creates a dilemma. On one hand, the American people clearly want their high schools to address many goals simultaneously (Goodlad, 1984). The comprehensive ideal asserts that each goal is legitimate for some set of students and that each school should have the internal capacity to help students meet those goals—high schools should be all things to all students. Thus, the assumption is that a wide range of interests, aptitudes, and levels of achievement obtains within *each* school (Conant, 1959). Not only is the comprehensive ideal generally permissive, but it also provides little guidance as to whether schools with very different students should develop different definitions of effectiveness.

On the other hand, a progressive specialization of high school populations has occurred in recent years (Abramowitz and Rosenfeld, 1978). In urban areas, the creation of magnet and other special-purpose schools worsens already-present segregation by achievement, income, and race (Luchs, 1986). Suburban schools often serve students similar to one another in terms of family background, aspirations, and abilities. This "homogenization" makes achievement of the comprehensive ideal meaningless because in many cases the variety of students assumed by that ideal is simply not present. Should all high schools be expected to reach towards the same comprehensive ideal, or should schools with large populations of especially high- or low-achieving students be expected to attain different standards? Is the comprehensive ideal an anachronism? And how would tampering with that socially driven and largely unexamined assumption about high schools be greeted? Although few bold experiments have been risked, there are some indications that parents will respond negatively to efforts to break with conventional patterns of school organization in order to provide instruction customized for large groups of low-achieving students (Metz, 1986). Yet it becomes difficult to justify advanced courses in calculus, physics, English literature, and foreign languages if there are too few students to take them.

One result of this societal ambiguity is that the comprehensive ideal is espoused in the rhetoric about schools while grounded, emergent definitions of effectiveness vary substantially from school to school. This variation is illustrated by the three schools in this study. In Somerville, the prevailing definition focused on the creation of good citizens by emphasizing preparation for the world or work and order. Implicit in the first criterion was an assumption about the school's clientele: its working-class students would be employed, and most would not go on to college or to higher-status, white-collar jobs. In effect, Somerville did not try to be a fully comprehensive high school. Instead, it concentrated its efforts on meeting the needs of the majority of its students.

The second criterion—order—is very different from what is frequently discussed as an educational "goal." Most discussions of goals refer to the characteristics that one would expect students to have when they graduate; they are future-oriented outcomes. However, there is another whole realm of goals referring to what the quality of life in schools should be like today. What role should these present-oriented goals play in thinking about school effectiveness? Should they be treated as ends or means? Some observers have been critical of educators for a kind of goal displacement in which present states are given more importance than future learning. Willower and Landis (1970), in particular, suggest that a concern for order becomes an end in itself for teachers and displaces a concern about instruction. Whatever the specific objective, the Somerville case study suggests that present-oriented goals specifying what desirable quality of life is can be an important element of effectiveness for people who work in schools.

Criteria of effectiveness at Westtown also emphasized present-oriented concerns, but of a very different character. For most Westtown teachers, the classroom was the "capitol"— that is, instructional matters had to take precedence over bureaucratic or political concerns when decisions were made. Order was to be maintained in a fair, consistent manner—but as an aid to good teaching, not as an end in itself—and the principal was expected to protect teachers from outside interference. As long as these criteria were met, the teachers viewed the school as effective. This definition of effectiveness gave each teacher considerable leeway to define the appropriate outcomes of schooling and required no agreement on what those outcomes should be. However, district administrators held an outcome-oriented definition of effectiveness that stressed achievement as measured on standardized tests.

Disagreement about definitions of effectiveness was the hallmark of Monroe. If there was any unity among teachers, it was related to a present-oriented concern—their desire to specialize. This teacher specialization was a typical by-product and necessary part of the comprehensive ideal. Its effect for teachers was to allow them to define an effective school as one that let them determine their criteria for instructional success. This belief enabled teachers to hold diverse conceptions of appropriate instructional outcomes without conflict. Teachers who held the academic perspective emphasized the development of higher-order cognitive skills, the knowledge presented in the academic classes, and college placement. Vocational teachers stressed the preparation of specific skills needed in the adult world. Those with the psychological development perspective advocated adjustment to the adult world in terms of a positive self-concept and self-control. The superintendent disrupted the coexistence of these diverse definitions by imposing his own definition of effectiveness on all teachers. This definition, like that of the Westtown administrators, valued the demonstration through test scores of increased basic skills learning.

Diversity in culturally shared beliefs about effectiveness is a mixed blessing. On the positive side, it permits a reasonable adjustment to the local context. Thus, the Somerville faculty, with support from its community, accommodated to the bulk of its working-class clientele, who intended to go directly from high school to work. The process definition of effectiveness at Westtown gave teachers license to be creative. On the negative side, such diversity permitted teaching that was stifling and inhumane. The strong and pervasive preparation-for-work orientation at Somerville stifled those students who might have wanted to go to college and seek higher-status careers. The inappropriate application of the academic perspective in Monroe allowed teachers to belittle students, to ignore their potential, and to generally abdicate a real responsibility to teach skills and knowledge that those students needed.

APPROPRIATE DEFINITIONS OF EFFECTIVENESS

In recent years, there have been attempts to develop rigorous definitions of effectiveness for American high schools and to insure that they are applied in a uniform and standardized way. For the most part, these standards focus on a limited set of outcomes, usually measured through achievement or other standardized tests. Beginning before the recent round of commission and blue ribbon panel reports and continuing at an accelerated pace since then, state legislatures have mandated stricter standards for high school graduation by requiring minimum competency tests or by increasing the number of required courses in specific subject areas as conditions of graduation. Forty-three states are considering or have recently passed legislation to tighten graduation standards (*Education Week,* 1985).

The research conducted in the three high schools offers a perspective for viewing these reform efforts and other attempts to stipulate definitions of effectiveness for high schools. Although the situation is clearly complex, and we do not pretend to have a complete answer, we do offer a number of suggestions.

First, any stipulative definition of high school effectiveness should be multifaceted. There is no easy solution to the problem of choosing among perhaps competing criteria, but the quality of life and education in schools seems to suffer when excessive attention is given to any *one* criterion to the exclusion of others. This is especially true when the criterion is achievement test results, such as the school's average SAT score, or the number of students passing a mandated minimum competency test. These criteria may be important as indicators of some kinds of achievement but should not stand alone as ways of judging a school's effectiveness. Achievement criteria should be combined with nonachievement outcomes like preparing students for work and citizenship roles as well as present-oriented concerns about quality of life. Quality-of-life criteria are also important because teachers, students, and administrators spend so much time on the job, and it is reasonable to expect that time to be at least a decent, and preferably a pleasant, experience.

Although we advocate multifaceted definitions of effectiveness, we do not expect all criteria to be equally well articulated. Since many definitions of effectiveness are implicit in school cultures, some criteria will be explicit and others tacit. As in Westtown, beliefs about what is true and good may not be verbalized and clarified until they are violated, but they are apparent in the rituals, routines, and day-to-day interactions in the school.

Second, as a standard that touches both present and future concerns, the quality of teaching observed in West-town—good, creative, responsive—ought to be a general criterion of school effectiveness. Creative teaching is, of course, a way to promote student learning as well as to foster a positive, respectful climate for everyone in the school. Searching for ways to improve one's craft is a way to keep teachers mentally alert and stimulated by their work, and interested teachers are interesting teachers who will make life more stimulating for students and others in the school. The kind of professionalism expressed in Westtown creates an exciting and vibrant work place that can be motivating for teachers and students.

Third, the concern for order is one of the universals in all schools, but order cannot be an end in itself. When it is, as happens in Somerville, it tends to be oppressive and stultifying. Moreover, a concern for order among students can permit the kind of abuse of power observed in Monroe, where some teachers insulted and belittled students. From our perspective, one criterion of an effective school should be that teachers and students respect each other and are decent to one another.

Such standards should apply not only to students but also to teachers. Unfortunately, in many high schools across the land, teachers degrade and humiliate students, often unwittingly. In our conception of an effective school, they would not do so.

Fourth, *appropriate* expectations for intellectual outcomes must be established. Since the effective schools movement, there has been a great interest in establishing "high" expectations. For Edmonds (1979) and others, high expectations meant the belief that all students could and would learn certain minimum basic skills. In high schools, especially among academically oriented teachers, high expectations can mean that students should be learning such academic subjects as advanced mathematics, science, or English. This was certainly the case at Monroe. These expectations can be debilitating for teachers and frustrating for students. They often go hand in hand with "low" expectations, taking the form of the belief that since students cannot learn what the teacher wants to teach, they cannot learn anything worthwhile. At this point we have a better sense of what appropriate expectations are not than what they are. At a minimum, however, it seems clear that a criterion of intellectual and academic effectiveness should be adjusted to the current capacities of students.

One way to state this criterion is for the school to take students from where they are as far as they can go. This criterion emphasizes *growth* rather than absolute levels of achievement. It has the added advantage of not giving schools credit or blame for the quality of student inputs. Although we have learned in the recent past that schools can make a substantial contribution to student learning, family background is still a major contributor to student achievement (Rowan, Bossert, and Dwyer, 1983). When schools are judged by levels of achievement rather than by how much students have learned while enrolled, the school's real contribution to learning is masked. With a growth-oriented definition of intellectual effectiveness, schools can neither take credit for the accomplishments of students who enter well prepared for academic tasks nor be stigmatized because of students who present greater instructional challenges.

A growth criterion has implications for schoolwide planning. On the one hand, it suggests that variation in program and staffing is needed to adjust to the central tendency of the school population. Thus, a school with a large low-achieving population requires a larger proportion of reading teachers than English teachers, and a school sending many children to college may need several teachers for gifted students. By this definition, it was sensible for Somerville to have a large business department since that unit provided training that was directly relevant to the futures that many students anticipated. On the other hand, it made little sense to allocate responsibility for basic skills instruction to only a quarter of the faculty at Monroe when the need for teachers to attend to those skills was so widespread.

When thinking about intellectual development, it is also important to differentiate between the needs of the large majority of students and those of the "outliers." Who those outliers are will vary, sometimes considerably, from school to school. In Somerville, insufficient attention was given to preparing students for college. At Monroe individual teachers initiated courses for such students, but there was little overall planning for the precollegiate group because there was so much emphasis on helping students pass the state tests. Teachers and administrators need to think more systematically about how to provide appropriate instruction for the students who are different from whatever is typical in that school.

Finally, the diversity in local definitions of effectiveness that we have observed is not only inevitable; it is also a good thing and should be encouraged. Diversity is inevitable because local definitions develop out of the nature of the student clientele, community expectations, and the history and culture of the specific institution. If diversity were valued more highly, schools could be more self-conscious about identifying the needs of various groups of students and planning for them rather than maintaining the trappings of the comprehensive high school because "that's how it's done." Our analysis leads us to conclude that reform efforts should encourage schools to reflect their local contexts, histories, and organizational cultures. This effort must be balanced by notions of what is good—criteria of effectiveness, or beliefs about the way things ought to be—that respect the individual while challenging him or her to change, grow, and develop competence as a functioning member of society.

Appendix

RESEARCH METHODS

A cultural perspective on the study of planned change in high schools suggests the need for research methods designed to explore participants' experiences and to view the organizational world as they do. To study cultures in this manner, an intensive fieldwork approach was used. In addition, only three high schools were selected for the case study. For each high school, a researcher spent at least thirty days in the site to gain an in-depth understanding of the school staff's norms, beliefs, and values as well as how change processes interplayed with them. A second fieldworker provided supplementary data collection at the Westtown site. This approach allowed sufficient time to get beneath the surface of the school's culture, to observe behavior, to become familiar with and to teachers, and to understand the subtleties and nuances of meanings that staff members attached to various actions and events. The primary data collection techniques were in-depth, open-ended interviewing and observing of teachers, students, and administrators in a variety of settings. To supplement these techniques, several types of documents were collected at each school.

A major consideration of the study was the responses of

the high school professionals to change and the processes used to implement it. Fullan (1982) makes a convincing case for understanding the perspectives of various actors in the change process, and he regards teachers as the most important group of actors. He notes that educational change is multidimensional, involving alternations in beliefs, teaching approaches, or materials (p. 30), and can have profound effects on teachers' "occupational identity, their sense of competence, and their self concept" (p. 33).

Data collection focused on how teachers and other professionals interpreted events and behaviors related to the change under way at each school, both proposed and actual; data analysis attempted to depict how each school's professional culture affected and was affected by efforts toward change. This appendix describes the research approach, the site selection, the data collection plan, and the data analysis strategy.

RESEARCH APPROACH

The research approach had two major features. First, it relied on one researcher per site, with the exception of Westtown. We originally expected to use two researchers per site but found that other constraints precluded this plan. Reliance on one person allowed that researcher to know the high school in greater depth than if the allotted time had been shared, although the value of two researchers cannot be disputed. What we lost in terms of validity checks we gained in increased sensitivity (Patton, 1980). The second major feature of the design was the selection of only three high schools. With this small number, it was possible to move beyond the idiosyncrasies of a single site and still capture the subtleties of the interaction between culture and change. The rationale for intensive fieldwork, in-depth knowledge by one researcher, and a limited number of sites was the same: each feature of the research approach encouraged detailed understanding of a high school's culture and maximized the opportunities to understand its implications for change initiatives.

The primary data collection technique was in-depth, open-ended interviews (Taylor and Bogdan, 1984). With teachers, these sessions often took place in classrooms, occasionally after the researcher viewed the person teach. The interview would initially attend to teaching, its purposes, and larger issues affecting the occupation. The focus eventually shifted to detailed cultural beliefs and specific efforts toward change. This shift rarely occurred in a single interview. Rather, as the relationship between the researcher and the school became more defined, the interviews became more introspective. Interviews with administrators tended to be more frequent primarily because we often checked in with them on each visit and they frequently inquired about the research. Because the schools were undergoing change while we were there, events were so fresh in people's minds that reconstructing the flow of events and people's reactions was relatively easy. We tried to trace the development of efforts toward change as perceived by the professional staff. We were particularly interested in their perspectives: how they viewed events, their responses to and interpretations of those events, and how they negotiated with the formal leaders, champions of change, and among themselves to create an emergent orientation toward change.

The secondary data collection technique was observation. We observed teachers teaching and then talked with them to understand their actions; we also shadowed administrators and discussed their actions. This approach has been used by Metz (1978) and McNeil (1981) to uncover significant cultural norms. We observed department meetings; full faculty meetings; parent-teacher association meetings; informal interactions in teachers' lounges, hallways, cafeterias, and department offices: formal ceremonies such as graduation exercises; and rites and rituals such as staff luncheons, tryouts for graduation speaker, and initial baseball team orientations.

This process of participant observation permitted the researcher to "hang around" the schools. This continual presence encouraged each researcher to get to know the individual school in some depth, fostered participation in a variety of activities, and familiarized participants with the researcher. Teachers and administrators felt much more willing to freely share their thoughts, doubts, hunches, and suspicions with a familiar and nonthreatening face. Through this intensive knowledge of the school, each researcher collected a variety of data on each emerging theme, thereby triangulating data from one source with another (Patton, 1980; Taylor and Bogdan, 1984; Denzin, 1970). This approach strengthened the development of themes and conclusions about the school.

In-depth interviewing and observing, in addition to fostering the collection of a variety of data, also encouraged participants to discuss (and, in some instances, discover) the more subtle aspects of their organizational worlds. Open-ended, free-flowing formal and informal interviewing created an atmosphere in which participants felt free to tell their stories—to share quite openly their perceptions of the school and others in it. Observing a variety of events, interactions, and processes also fostered this subtle display of deeply held, often tacitly expressed values and norms.

Through the interviews and observations, the researchers traced teachers' interpretations of efforts toward change and focused on the dynamics of those complex processes. In exploring teachers' perspectives, we identified some forces that staff members saw as preserving the established order and as pushing for change. Norms having a sacred quality were under dispute in all three sites, and this dispute created conflict, anger, and frustration. We documented these occurrences, identified their initiators, and traced the spread of commitment to or dispute about them.

We anticipated and found variance within the teacher group. Salient subcultural groups were evident at each school. This was expected because although the study of cultures is the study of shared meanings, "the degree of sharedness is, of course, variable and dependent upon the relative power of individuals and groups acting in a social field" (Goldberg, 1984:160). Metz (1978), for example, identified two broad categories of teachers based on their values and beliefs—their philosophies of teaching. In a different study, Metz (1982) once again found two salient teacher groups, but this time the distinction was based on reactions to and beliefs about schoolwide change.

SITE SELECTION

The original research design called for the selection of two to four improving high schools for the project. For this selection process, we formulated a definition of an improving school, contacted informants and asked for nominations of improving schools, visited each school to ascertain if there was some evidence of improvement and if there was interest in participating in the study, selected a short list of schools, and negotiated final entry.

The definition of improvement was intentionally very broad in order to include a wide range of change processes. This definition included the following:

1. The school could be getting better in a number of areas, including instruction, achievement, order and discipline, attendance, or climate.
2. The change might or might not involve a special improvement effort or the "adoption of an innovation" or new teaching approaches.
3. The school did not need to be exemplary, although exemplary schools were not precluded; what was crucial was some real evidence that things were getting better.

Although the schools could vary in a number of ways, we looked for evidence for the following:

1. The school had actually improved in whatever area school staff members said they had seen improvement over the last two or three years. It was not enough to be involved in programs; there had to be demonstrable results in a quantitative form.

2. The evidence of change had to include evidence that students were behaving differently or learning more.
3. The change had to be schoolwide and not limited to a single department, grade level, or small group.

Special emphasis was placed on finding improving schools that were in urban settings. For cost reasons, it was also important to identify schools within driving distance of our office.

To obtain nominations, we contacted the following organizations:

1. The Middle State Association of Colleges and Schools: Commission on Secondary Schools
2. Bucks County Intermediate Unit (Pennsylvania)
3. Chester County Intermediate Unit (Pennsylvania)
4. Pennsylvania Elementary and Secondary Principals' Association
5. Philadelphia School District
6. Camden County Office of the New Jersey Department of Education
7. Gloucester County Office of the New Jersey Department of Education
8. Burlington County Office of the New Jersey Department of Education
9. Educational Information Resource Center (formerly EIC-South)

In each organization, we provided informants with background on the study's purposes and indicated that we would follow up with nominees to obtain additional data. We asked for suggestions and descriptive information on the nominated schools. In addition to working through these nine agencies, personal contacts and the knowledge of other Research for Better Schools (RBS) staff were employed.

Through this process, fourteen high schools were identified as potential candidates for the study. In each case, the principal or superintendent was telephoned. Thirteen agreed to discuss the study further. In each meeting, the study's

Table 1

Demographic Data for Three High School Sites

Item	Westtown (grades 7–12)	Monroe (grades 9–12)	Sommerville (grades 9–12)
Enrollment	1,000	800	1,500
Percent minority	05	95	45
District enrollment	2,000	4,000	213,000
City size	16,000	41,000	3,000,000
City growth pattern	Decline	Stable	Stable

purposes, research activities, and feedback to the school were described, and questions were answered. In addition, we asked about the nature of improvements in the school and for evidence that student behavior or learning had changed in a positive direction. This evidence usually took the form of several years of records, including achievement test scores, SAT scored, minimum competency test scores, attendance data, and lateness rates, depending on the claim to improvement made by the principal.

The data were reviewed by RBS staff, and three schools were selected for inclusion in the study. Table 1 provides some demographic information on each one.

Westtown High School served a white-collar suburban community that was becoming progressively more blue-collar. The community had a historical interest in maintaining a good high school that may now be somewhat declining. The district's leadership was stable; the same superintendent had served for a number of years. The high school had had a good reputation in the region for some time, especially as a school with a positive learning climate. However, in the early 1980s, declining SAT scores raised the possibility that the quality of the academic program was slipping. A new principal was hired in 1982 with a mandate to improve the academic program, and he took a number of steps to tighten the curriculum and emphasize academics. The history of composite SAT scores for the high school indicates that measured achievement improved over the last two years:

Year	Composite SAT score
1978	918
1979	914
1980	933
1981	913
1982	879
1983	901
1984	916

RBS staff members first visited Westtown High School in the spring of 1984. We met with the principal and department heads. The department heads expressed some concerns about the study, but these were worked out over the summer, and an agreement to participate was reached.

Monroe High School was the only high school in a small city with a declining industrial base. Recent achievement scores had been low throughout the district. Five years ago a new superintendent was hired who was committed to a forceful approach to school improvement. He had sought the assistance of Research for Better Schools (RBS), and one RBS program was providing training and assistance in the high school. In the last two years a new principal was hired to oversee improvement efforts in the high school. The success of those efforts is apparent in the following statistics in Table 2.

When we approached the superintendent early in the fall

Table 2

Indicators of Improvement at Monroe High School

Year	Average daily attendance %	Percent passing state minimum competency test (9th Grade) Communication	Math	CAT grade point equivalent 10th Grade Reading	Math	12th Grade Reading	Math
81	77	61	55	8.7	9.0	11.0	10.0
82	83	70	74	8.6	8.9	11.2	11.2
83	84	70	70	9.0	10.0	10.9	11.0
84	85	82	78	9.3	10.0	11.2	11.6

of 1984, he was eager to participate in the study; administrative approval was quickly granted. However, it soon became apparent that there was considerable tension between the administration and a substantial portion of the high school teachers. It seemed likely that the study would meet with resistance strong enough to seriously impede data collection unless unusual steps were taken. For that reason, we approached the teachers' collective bargaining unit separately and asked for its approval of the study in hopes of alleviating this resentment. When that unit raised no serious objection to participation in the study, fieldwork was initiated.

Somerville High School was located in a major urban metropolis in the mid-Atlantic region. It served a blue-collar working class neighborhood and was very closely knit. Parents, uncles, aunts, and cousins of many students had graduated from Somerville, and community involvement in the school was high. As one of eighteen comprehensive high schools in the city, Somerville responded to both district (citywide) and subdistrict (area) administrative structures. The school was confronted by a new district superintendent who had recently implemented a standardized curriculum and strict eligibility and promotion requirements and a state mandate for new high school graduation requirements. Six years ago, a new principal came to Somerville and began to turn the school around. His first initiatives were broad, but at the heart of his activity was a commitment to (1) discipline and attendance, and (2) building school spirit. The following data reveal how attendance and lateness improved:

Year	Percent in attendance	Percent late
1980	78.3	5.8
1981	73.7	6.9
1982	77.8	4.8
1982	82.2	4.0
1984	85.4	3.8

RBS staff members first visited Somerville in the summer of 1984 and met with the principal for initial discussions about the research. We returned on three separate occasions, once to meet with the acting principal, a second time to meet with the building committee, and a third time to present the study to the faculty as a whole. Although some questions were raised, Somerville agreed to participate. Fortunately, shortly after the onset of fieldwork, the principal returned from medical leave.

DATA COLLECTION PLAN

The data collection activities reflected the uniqueness of the three different settings. In Westtown and Somerville, building trust with the participants went quite smoothly and easily, whereas at Monroe some tension and suspicion remained throughout the study. Data collection at Monroe relied on formally setting up interview sessions and scheduling site visits. At both Westtown and Somerville, the researchers were welcome to come and go as they pleased and to approach staff casually. Table 3 lists the number of days, interviews conducted, and hours of observation at each high school.

    To guide data collection, we identified those *events, settings, actors,* and *artifacts* (Miles and Huberman, 1984) that had the greatest potential to yield good data on cultural beliefs. These items provided parameters to guide data collection, whether we were observing or interviewing. First we focused on *settings,* or places in the school where salient staff interaction occurred. During the first few weeks in the field, we collected data in the following settings:

> Public places (main office, hallways, parking lot)
> Teachers' lounge or lunchroom
> Classrooms
> private offices
>> Counsellor's
>> Disciplinarian's
>> Vice principal's for scheduling
>> Coaches'
>> Principal's

Table 3

**Data Collection Activities at Westtown, Monroe, and
Somerville High School**

Activity	Westtown	Monroe	Somerville
Site visit days	57	30	40
Interviews			
Teachers/counselors/	85	57	64
librarians	(92	(82	(84
	possible)	possible)	possible)
Administrators	4	5	4
Support staff	0	5	3
District office	1	4	0
Parents	0	0	8
Observations			
Total hours on site	200	130	195
Number of classrooms	36	41	42
Informal conversations	94	61	121
Meetings			
Department	0	1	5
Full faculty	3	5	1
Parent association	0	0	1
Department chairpersons	9	1	0
Other special committees	2	0	4
School Board	1	0	0
Parent-teacher night	0	1	0

Department office or work room
Gymnasium or locker room
Auditorium
Meeting rooms

In each of these settings, certain *events* occurred that we
wanted to observe and talk about with people. For example, in
the disciplinarian's office took place the handling of routine
infractions, suspensions, and expulsions; in the counselor's
office were crisis interventions. Both types of events revealed
beliefs about the school, the nature of the work, and how

people should relate to one another and treat students. In general, the events included the following:

Events in which professionals interacted
    Formal routines: faculty/department meetings, evaluations, union meetings
    Informal routines: lunch/coffee breaks//recess, morning arrivals
Events in which professionals interacted with students
    Teaching acts
    Extracurricular activities: sporting events, drama productions, music rehearsals
    Suspensions and expulsions
    Roster changes
    Crisis (such as drug use) counseling
    Assemblies and pep rallies

The first category of events provided major data on teachers' deeply held beliefs about their work and the overall purposes of teaching in general and the school in particular. Faculty and department meetings were important and primarily entailed observation. As teachers discussed curriculum, testing, new state requirements, homework policies, and the more mundane aspects of high school life (such as announcements of schedule change, field trips, and time fillers), their beliefs about teaching and norms regarding how they should relate to one another in a meeting setting became apparent.

Morning routines and other informal encounters also revealed these values and beliefs, but in less structured ways. Brief encounters involved requests for help, plans for meeting, supportive gestures, and queries about how a particular concept or skill was best taught—events in which professionals and students interacted—and provided data about how adults and students were expected to relate to one another. Both in the classroom and when teachers and students interacted, these encounters revealed whether there was a sense of caring or of community, what teachers expectations were for one another regarding behavior and achievement, and what teachers felt was their overriding mission.

As data collection progressed, we tried to understand the perspectives of the following *actors:*

Administrators
  Principal
  Vice principal for discipline
  Vice principal for curriculum
  Vice Principal for schedule/roster
Counsellors
Coaches
Teachers
  Department heads
  Different tenure in building
  Different departments
Students
  Different ability levels
  Different visibility (that is, participation in extracurricu-
    lar Activities)
External actors
  Superintendents
  Curriculum coordinators
  Board members
  Community members
  State education agencies

Finally, we observed and, where appropriate, collected certain artifacts that provided additional data. Included were the following:

Documents
  School newspapers
  Policy statements
  Attendance records
  Disciplinary records
  Achievement test scores
Objects
  Logos
  Mascots
  Trophies

Decorations
Physical arrangements

The emphasis was on observation in the data collection activities because many facets of culture are implicit, subtle, and tacit. Our approach was to infer norms and values from behavior patterns and from conversations. Interviews helped us understand the settings and reconstruct the history of efforts toward change in each school. Interviewing was also a necessary part of legitimizing our presence.

The following schedule provides a sample day in the field and demonstrates how settings, events, and actors were covered.

Period	Activity
1	Observe disciplinarians' office—"getting into school" processes—lateness procedures, morning activities
2	Interview disciplinarians
3	Observe in teachers' lounge
4	Interview department head
5	Observe lunchroom activities
6	Observe lunchroom activities
7	Observe classroom
8	Interview teacher
9	Catch breath/write field notes

After school—observe sports, rehearsals—coaches and students

This schedule served as an initial guide to insure that we became known to key department heads and to regular teachers in each department. It also helped establish that observations—"hanging around"—would be a regular part of each day. As we moved along in Westtown and Somerville, observation became more important; later interviews were designed to test emerging hypotheses or to assess the distribution of adherence to particular beliefs and norms.

DATA ANALYSIS

Data analysis is the process of bringing meaning to a mass of detailed information. It involves categorizing the data, interpreting them, and verifying that they do in fact meaningfully reflect the phenomenon chosen for study (Taylor and Bogdan, 1984; Patton, 1980).

The data analysis strategy was designed as a cross-case comparison approach (Yin, 1984): that is, the data from each site were summarized, categorized, and interpreted apart from the data from the other sites; grounded case studies were written from each high school, reflecting that particular school's unique story. These cases were then shared and compared, the analytic task being to identify common themes and/or patterns and areas of difference in beliefs and values or in responses to the efforts toward change. The final analytic task was to build a plausible explanation for the data at all three sites—to build a grounded theory accounting for the consequences of the interplay of cultural content and efforts toward change.

Categorizing voluminous pages of field notes is tedious work. It is this task, however, that determines how much of the data eventually is used in subsequent arguments and descriptions. As fieldwork wound down, we began to identify important themes and phenomena that were emerging in the respective sites. These discussions, as well as the original design for the study, led each researcher to devise a coding scheme that was both appropriate for his or her site and that had the potential for enabling cross-site comparisons. For example, for Westtown, four categories of codes were created: (1) "sacred and profane," (2) "staff leaving/health/uncertainty about future," (3) "description of the quality of staff interactions," and (4) "similarity of expressions of ideas and language." These emerged as salient categories during data collection and discussions with the research team. Under them the multitude of discrete data bits coalesced into themes. The first code included statements about willingness to change in certain areas as well as indications of what people felt the place stood for and what the purpose of their work was; the second catalogued the array and magnitude of malignant conditions staff reported; the third captured comparisons between the "Camelot" of the past and the current relationships among teachers and administrators; and the fourth collated data on the considerable uniformity of the teacher culture in the school. From these themes, then, a more coherent picture of the school could be built. Every interview, observation, and written thought was reviewed and coded. This work in turn provided a ready index of supporting and contradictory evidence of the interpretive activity that followed.

Interpreting the data goes hand in hand with data collection and categorization. The interpretive act gives meaning to observed events and recorded words; it begins with the original conceptualization of a study and ends with the final editing of the written report.

The credibility of the data was insured through three design decisions: (1) long-term engagement in the field to overcome bias, (2) sharing and critiquing the case study analyses by the other members of the research team, and (3) soliciting feedback from two external researchers and by participants at each of the sites. At Westtown, feedback from participants at the school went quite smoothly, with teachers and administrators taking an interest in the analysis and corroborating many of the interpretations. At Monroe the teachers who reviewed the report were generally in agreement about the findings, although they were surprised at the importance given to negative attitudes toward the students. The superintendent viewed the report as a confirmation of his views. At Somerville, when a draft of the report was shared with the school's administrators, a few of the findings were challenged as not reflecting the school or individuals in it. The central themes were, however, corroborated. In Monroe and Somerville, the research team used these reactions as expressions of each school's values about the research process.

The verification process had two aspects. First, during data collection, we had to insure an adequate sample of events, settings, and actors to be sure we had not sampled an idiosyncratic pocket of the universe. This we insured by getting to know the departments (as formal structures) and the informal social groups, and by allocating adequate time to the site (Patton, 1980). Second, as themes and hypotheses became evident in the data, we tested the ideas out (as described above) against each other, study participants, and outside experts. Moreover, in each setting, formal feedback was provided. In two sites, copies of the case studies included in this report were shared with key individuals; in the third, a summary was provided. This process allowed participants to react, critique, and discuss the interpretations and conclusions made.

The processes of data analysis used in the study maximized understanding of the complexity of each individual high school. The research was guided by a common set of assumptions and concepts. These processes encouraged the finely textured descriptions developed in the case studies and prompted the set of propositions and theoretical statements developed in the concluding chapter. A more tightly constrained analysis would have been the death knell of these ethnographic accounts of life in high schools.

References

Abramowitz, S., & Rosenfeld, S. (1978). *Declining enrollment: The challenge for the coming decade.* Washington, D.C.: National Institute of Education.

Berger, P. L. (1967). *The sacred canopy.* Garden City, NY: Anchor.

Berman, P. E. (1981). Toward an implementation paradigm. In R. Lehming and M. Kane (Eds.), *Improving schools: Using what we know.* Beverly Hills, CA: Sage.

Berman, P. E., & McLauglin, M. W. (1977). *Federal programs supporting educational change,* Vol. VII: *Factors affecting implementation and continuation.* Santa Monica, CA: Rand.

Boyer, E. L. (1983). *High school: A report on secondary education in America.* New York: Harper & Row.

Breer, P. E., & Locke, E. A. (1965). *Task experience as a source of attitudes.* Homewood, IL: Dorsey.

Brim, O. G., & Wheeler, S. (1966). *Socialization after childhood.* New York: Wiley.

Brookover, W. B. (1979). *School social systems and student achievement: Schools can make a difference.* New York: Praeger.

Brown, R. H. (1978). Bureaucracy as praxis. *Administrative Science Quarterly, 23,* 365–382.

Bucher, R., & Stelling, J. (1977). *Becoming professional.* London: Sage.

Changing course: A 50 state survey of reform measures. (1985, February 6). *Education Week*, p. 11.

Clark, B. L. (1970). *The distinctive college: Antioch, Reed, and Swarthmore*. Chicago: Aldine.

Clark, D. L., & Astuto, T. A. (1984). Effective schools and school improvement: A comparative analysis of two lines of inquiry. *Educational Administration Quarterly, 20*(3), 41–68.

Clark, D. L., Lotto, L. S., & McCarthy, M. M. (1980). Factors associated with success in urban elementary schools. *Phi Delta Kappan, 61*(7), 467–470.

Coch, L., & French, J. R. P. (1968). Overcoming resistance to change. In D. Cartwright & A. Zander (Eds.), *Group dynamics*. New York: Harper & Row.

Cohen, D. K., & Neufeld, B. (1981). The failure of the high school and the progress of education. *Daedalus, 110*(3), 69–90.

Coleman, J. S. (1966). *Equality of educational opportunity*. Washington, D.C.: U.S. Government Printing Office.

Conant, J. B. (1959). *The American high school today: A first report to interested citizens*. New York: McGraw Hill.

Corbett, H. D., Dawson, J. L., & Firestone, W. A. (1984). *School context and school change*. New York: Teachers College Press.

Corbett, H. D., & Rossman, G. B. (1986). Local conditions and local leadership for implementing change. Paper presented at the annual meeting of the American Educational Research Association, San Francisco.

Crandall, D. P., Eiseman, J. W., & Louis, K. L. (1986). Strategic planning issues that bear on the success of school improvement efforts. *Educational Administration Quarterly, 22*, 21–53.

Crandall, D. P., & Loucks, S. F. (1983). *People, policies, and practices: Examining the chain of school improvement, Vol. X: A roadmap for school improvement*. Andover, MA: The Network.

Cusick, P. A. (1983). *The egalitarian ideal and the American high school: Studies of three schools*. New York: Longman.

Deal, T. E. (1985). The symbolism of effective schools. *The Elementary School Journal, 85*(3), 601–620.

Deal, T. E., & Kennedy, A. A. (1982). *Corporate cultures: The rites and rituals of corporate life.* Reading, MA: Addison-Wesley.

Denzin, N. K. (1970). *The research act: A theoretical introduction to sociological methods.* New York: Aldine.

Dunn, W. N., & Swierczek, F. W. (1977). Planned organizational change: Toward grounded theory. *Journal of Applied Behavioral Science, 13,* 135–158.

Durkheim, E. (1965). *The elementary forms of religious life.* New York: Free Press.

Edmonds, R. (1979). Effective schools for the urban poor. *Educational Leadership, 37*(1), 15–24.

Eliade, M. (1959). *The sacred and the profane.* New York: Harcourt, Brace, & World.

Fine, G. A. (1984). Negotiated orders and organizational cultures. *Annual Review of Sociology, 10,* 239–262.

Firestone, W. A., & Corbett, H. D. (1987). Planned organizational change. In N. Boyan (Ed.), *Handbook of Research on Educational Administration.* New York: Longman.

Fullan, M. (1985). Change processes and strategies at the local level. *Elementary School Journal, 85*(3), 391–422.

———. (1982). *The meaning of educational change.* New York: Teachers College Press.

Giaquinta, J. B. (1973). The process of organizational change in schools. In F. N. Kerlinger (Ed.), *Review of research in education* (Vol. 1). Itasca, IL: Peacock.

Goldberg, H. E. (1984). Evaluation, ethnography, and the concept of culture: Disadvantaged youth in an Israeli town. In D. M. Fetterman, (Ed.), *Ethnography in educational evaluation* (pp. 153–173). Beverly Hills, CA: Sage.

Goodlad, J. I. (1984). *A place called school.* New York: McGraw Hill.

Goodman, P. S., Pennings, J. M., and associates. (1977). *New perspectives on organizational effectiveness.* San Francisco: Jossey-Bass.

Gordon, D. (1984). *The myths of school self-renewal.* New York: Teachers College Press.

Gross, N., Giaquinta, J. B., & Bernstein, M. (1971). *Implementing organizational change.* New York: Basic Books.

Hall, G., et al. (1984). Effects of three principal styles on school improvement. *Educational Leadership, 41*(5), 22–29.

Hansen, J. F. (1979). *Sociocultural perspectives on human learning: An introduction to educational anthropology.* Englewood Cliffs, NJ: Prentice-Hall.

Herriott, R. E., & Firestone, W. A. (1984). Two images of schools as organizations: A refinement and extension. *Education Administration Quarterly, 20*(4), 41–57.

House, E. R. (1981). Three perspectives on educational innovation: Technological, political and cultural. In R. Lehming and M. Kane (Eds.), *Improving schools: Using what we know.* Beverly Hills, CA: Sage.

Huberman, M., & Miles, M. B. (1984). *Innovation up close: How school improvement works.* New York: Plenum.

Jackson, P. (1968). *Life in classrooms,* New York: Holt, Rinehart, and Winston.

James, T., & Tyack, D. (1983). Learning from past efforts to reform the high school. *Phi Delta Kappan, 64*(6), 400–406.

Kanengiser, A. (1985, October 15). Pay, future may run off professors. *USA Today.*

Kottkamp, R. B. (1984). The principal as cultural leader. *Planning and Changing, 15,* 152–160.

Lewin, K. (1952). Group decision and social change. In G. E. Swanson, T. E. Newcomb, and E. L. Hartley, (Eds.), *Readings in social psychology* (revised edition). New York: Holt, Rinehart, & Winston.

Lightfoot, S. L. (1983). *The good high school.* New York: Basic Books.

Lortie, D. (1975). *Schoolteacher.* Chicago: University of Chicago Press.

Luchs, K. (1986). *The zoned high school in Baltimore: Report and recommendations.* Baltimore, MD: Baltimore City Schools.

McNeil, L. M. (1981). Negotiating classroom knowledge: Beyond achievement and socialization. *Journal of Curriculum Studies, 13,* 313–328.

McPherson, G. H. (1979). What principals should know about teachers. In D. Erickson & T. Reller (Eds.), *The principal in metropolitan schools.* Berkeley, CA: McCutchan.

Manning, P. K. (1979). Metaphors of the field: Varieties of

organizational discourse. *Administrative Science Quarterly, 24,* 660–671.

Metz, M. H. (1986). *Different by design.* New York: Routledge & Kegan Paul.

———. (1982). Additional considerations about school organization and adolescent development. In F. M. Newmann, & C. E. Sleeter (Eds.), *Adolescent development and secondary schooling* (pp. 107–120). Madison, WI: Wisconsin Center for Education Research.

———. (1978). *Classrooms and corridors: The crisis of authority in desegregated secondary schools.* Berkeley, CA: University of California Press.

Meyer, J. W., & Rowan, B. (1977). Institutionalized organizations: Formal structure as myth and ceremony. *American Journal of Sociology, 83,* 340–363.

Miles, M. B. (1981). Mapping the common properties of schools. In R. Lehming & M. Kane (Eds.), *Improving schools: Using what we know.* Beverly Hills, CA: Sage.

Miles, M. B., & Huberman, A. M. (1984). *Qualitative data analysis: A sourcebook of new methods.* Beverly Hills: CA: Sage.

Mohr, L. B. (1982). *Explaining organizational behavior: The limits and possibilities of theory and research.* San Francisco: Jossey-Bass.

National Commission on Excellence in Education. (1983). *A nation at risk: The imperative for educational reform.* Washington, D.C.: U.S. Department of Education.

Patton, M. Q. (1980). *Qualitative evaluation methods.* Beverly Hills, CA: Sage.

Peters, T. J. (1980). Management systems: The language of organizational character and competence. *Organizational Dynamics, 9,* 3–26.

———. (1978). Symbols, patterns, and settings: An optimistic case for getting things done. *Organizational Dynamics, 7,* 3–23.

Peters, T. J., & Waterman, R. H. (1982). *In search of excellence: Lessons from America's best run companies.* New York: Harper & Row.

Pfeffer, J. (1981). Management as symbolic action: The creation and maintenance of organizational paradigms. In

L. L. Cummings & B. M. Staw (Eds.), *Research in organizational behavior* (Vol. 3). Greenwich, CT: JAI Press.

Pfeffer, J., & Lawler, J. (1980). Effects of job alternatives, extrinsic rewards, and behavioral commitment on attitudes toward the organization: A field test of the Insufficient Justification Paradigm. *Administrative Science Quarterly, 25,* 38–56.

Pfeffer, J., & Salancik, G. R. (1978). *The external control of organizations: A resource dependence perspective.* New York: Harper & Row.

Powell, A. G., Farrar, E., & Cohen, D. K. (1985). *The shopping mall high school: Winners and losers in the educational marketplace.* Boston: Houghton Mifflin.

Purkey, S. C., & Smith, M. S. (1983). Effective schools—A review. *Elementary School Journal, 83*(4), 427–452.

Rohlen, T. P. (1983). *Japan's high schools.* Berkeley, CA: University of California Press.

Rowan, B., Bossert, S. T., & Dwyer, D. C. (1983). Research on effective schools: A cautionary note. *Educational Researchers, 12*(4), 24–31.

Rutter, M., et al. (1979). *Fifteen thousand hours: Secondary schools and their effect on children.* Cambridge, MA: Harvard University Press.

Sarason, S. B. (1971). *The culture of the school and the problem of change.* Boston: Allyn & Bacon.

Schein, E. H. (1985). *Organizational culture and leadership.* San Francisco: Jossey-Bass.

Schlechty, P. C. (1976). *Teaching and social behavior: Toward an organizational theory of instruction.* Boston: Allyn & Bacon.

Scott, W. R. (1977). Effectiveness of organizational effectiveness studies. In P. S. Goodman, J. M. Pennings, and associates (Eds.), *New perspectives on organizational effectiveness.* San Francisco: Jossey-Bass.

Simpson, I. H. (1979). *From student to nurse.* Cambridge: Cambridge University Press.

Sizer, T. R. (1984). *Horace's compromise: The dilemma of the American high school.* Boston: Houghton Mifflin.

Stallings, J. (1985). A study of implementation of Madeline Hunter's model and its effects on students. *Journal of Educational Research, 78*(6), 325–337.

Taylor, S. J., & Bogdan, R. (1984). *Introduction to qualitative research methods: The search for meanings* (2nd edition). New York: Wiley.

Tichy, N. M. (1983). *Managing strategic change: Technical, political, and cultural dynamics.* New York: Wiley.

Ulrich, W. L. (1984). HRM and culture: History, ritual, and myth. *Human Resource Management, 23(2), 117–128.*

Wallace, A. F. C. (1970). *Culture and personality* (2nd edition). New York: Random House.

Watson, G. (1969). Resistance to change. In W. Bennis, K. Beene, & R. Chin (Eds.), *The planning of change* (2nd ed.). New York: Holt, Rinehart, & Winston.

Welch, W. W. (1979). Twenty years of science curriculum development: A look back. In D.C. Berliner (Ed.), *Review of research in education.* Washington, D.C.: AERA.

Wellisch, J. B., et al. (1978). School management and organization in successful schools (ESAA in-depth study of schools). *Sociology of Education, 51*(3), 21–26.

Williams, R. (1970). *American society: A sociological interpretation,* (3rd edition). New York: Knopf.

Willower, D. J., & Landis, C. A. (1970). Pupil control ideology and professional orientation of school faculty. *Journal of Secondary Education, 45*(3), 118–123.

Wilson, B. L., & Corbett, H. D. (1983). Organization and change: The effects of school linkages on the quantity of implementation. *Educational Administration Quarterly, 19*(4), 85–104.

Wilson, E. K. (1971). *Sociology: Rules, roles, and relationships.* Homewood, IL: Dorsey.

Wolcott, H. F. (1977). *Teachers vs. technocrats.* University of Oregon: Center for Educational Policy and Management.

Yin, R. K. (1984). *Case study research: Design and methods.* Beverly Hills, CA: Sage.

Zaltman, G., & Duncan, R. (1977). *Strategies for planned change.* New York: Wiley.

Zucker, L. G. (1977). The role of institutionalization in cultural persistence. *American Sociological Review, 42,* 726–743.

INDEX

Abramowitz, S., 37, 135
Accredidation, in Monroe, 34; in
  Westtown, 84–85
Administrator(s) authority, 17; as a
  buffer, 79–80, 88, 119; as leader, 18;
  and manipulating symbols, 94, 99,
  119, 129, 131; role in promoting
  change, 26, 28, 29, 44, 46, 47, 51,
  52–55, 56, 59, 60, 63, 76, 82,
  83–91, 94, 96, 98, 103, 106–107,
  119; turnover, 28, 82, 94, 95, 98–99,
  103, 115, 125, 127, 128, 130–132
Administrator-teacher relationship, *see*
  Teacher-administrator relationship
Astuto, T., 21

Behavioral change, 20, 26, 60;
  compared to cultural change, 4, 18,
  59, 129–132; strategies for, 4, 128
Berger, P., 11, 17
Berman, P., 12, 18, 131
Bernstein, M., 18, 20
Bogdan, R., 145, 146, 157
Bossert, S., 133, 140
Boyer, E., 36
Breer, P., 129
Brim, O., 128

Brookover, W., 122
Brown, R., 5
Bucher, R., 128

Change continuation, 132
Clark, B., 16, 58
Clark, D., 21
Coch, L., 19
Cohen, D., 36, 37, 57, 58, 135
Coleman, J., 122
Comprehensive high school, 6, 14, 25,
  36–39, 57–58, 94, 134–135, 141
Conant, J., 36, 37, 134, 135
Corbett, D., 2, 12, 62, 122, 131, 132
Crandall, D., 18, 20
Cultural change, 4, 13, 20, 23, 62, 90;
  compared to behavioral change, 4,
  18, 59, 129–132; likelihood of
  occurrence of, 130–131; three
  processes of, 13–17, 129
Culture, characteristics of, 13;
  definition of, 5; and language, 5–6;
  see Cultural change, Normative
  structure, Organizational culture,
  School culture
Curriculum alignment, 16, 45, 46–52,
  59, 127
Cusick P., 58

169

DATE DUE —

DEMCO